SpringerBriefs in Cybersecurity

For further volumes:
http://www.springer.com/series/10634

Rolf H. Weber · Ulrike I. Heinrich

Anonymization

Springer

Prof. Dr. Rolf H. Weber
Faculty of Law
University of Zurich
Zurich
Switzerland

Ulrike I. Heinrich
Faculty of Law
University of Zurich
Zurich
Switzerland

ISSN 2193-973X ISSN 2193-9748 (electronic)
ISBN 978-1-4471-4065-8 ISBN 978-1-4471-4066-5 (eBook)
DOI 10.1007/978-1-4471-4066-5
Springer London Heidelberg New York Dordrecht

Library of Congress Control Number: 2012936253

Printed on acid-free paper

Springer is part of Springer Science+Business Media (www.springer.com)

Contents

Abstract

Particularly within the last decade the Internet has developed as a phenomenon encompassing social, cultural, economic, and legal facets. Since it has become common practice to use the Internet for both retrieving and providing information it gained the position of a very valuable tool in everyday life. Contrary to many Internet participants' erroneous assumption of surfing on the Internet anonymously, unless disclosing their identity by entering private data, users leave data tracks on each website they pass. Accordingly, surfing on the World Wide Web is far from being an anonymous activity of no consequences. Hence, the decision not to make available personal data best protects the informational and communicative self-determination of the persons concerned since with the development of new technologies new attacking tools are regularly developed, too. For putting the netizens' wish for anonymous communication and the protection of their privacy in the online world into practice, in recent years a number of networking techniques have been innovated. With regard to the fact that these techniques are also misused for illegal activities since parallel to the information and communication technologies' development and the augmented use of the globally available World Wide Web as communication tool crimes and/or their preliminary measures increasingly shift from the real into the online world, on the one hand it is still a debatable point whether there is (or should be) a right to act anonymously on the Internet; on the other hand, governmental interventions into anonymity requests should only be legal if a sufficiently legitimized public interest is given.

Rolf H. Weber—Professor of civil, European and commercial law at the Law Faculty of the University of Zurich, Switzerland, and Visiting Professor at the University of Hong Kong, Kong Kong, attorney-at-law (Zurich).

Ulrike I. Heinrich—Attorney-at-law (Berlin), research assistant and PhD student at the University of Zurich.

Abstract

Chapter 1
Notion of Anonymity

1.1 Term and Meaning of Anonymity

Stemming from the Greek word "anonymia", the term anonymity/anonymous stands for "namelessness", "not identified" or "of unknown name" (Oxford Dictionaries) and usually bears on a person's appearance in public. Consequently, anonymity occurs if a person's identity being involved in a not-transparent/not disclosed process is non-determinable since the acting person remains unknown to the other acting entities or makes no appearance towards the other participants or acts within the anonymous process without recognizable name (Bundesamt für Sicherheit in der Informationstechnik 2001, Chap. 1).

However, anonymity does not necessarily presuppose the complete anonymousness of a person's identity or the lack of a name; even the unrenownedness of an individual's name could suffice (Brunst 2009, p. 7). In order to distinguish anonymity from undetectability, it is therefore imperative that one party vaguely knows about the existence of another party without knowing his/her complete identity (Wallace 1999, p. 25).

A further differentiation needs to be made towards pseudonymity which is characterized by the use of a false name even though this practice may lead to anonymity, too. Concerning this issue Froomkin distinguishes between four forms of identification, namely (1) traceable anonymity, (2) untraceable anonymity, (3) traceable pseudonymity and (4) untraceable pseudonymity (Froomkin 1995, para. 11): (1) In the case of communication by email Froomkin refers to traceable anonymity if the receiver of an email gets no information about the identity of the email's originator directly but could find it out by contacting the interconnected operator. (2) Compared with this, in the case of untraceable anonymity, the author of the email is unidentifiable at all. In respect of pseudonymity, Froomkin refers (4) to untraceable pseudonymity if the email's originator uses a false and untraceable identity and, in contrast, assumes (3) traceable pseudonymity if the used pseudonym can be traced back to the originator regardless of whether by the mail's recipient or by someone else.

R. H. Weber and U. I. Heinrich, *Anonymization*, SpringerBriefs in Cybersecurity,
DOI: 10.1007/978-1-4471-4066-5_1, © The Author(s) 2012

1.2 Underlying Motivations of Anonymity

Anonymous actions have a long history and "anonymous pamphlets, leaflets, brochures and even books have played an important role in the progress of mankind" (Solove 2007, p. 139).[1] Hence, the individuals' motivations of making an appearance without revealing their identity are manifold. The intentions range from legal, legitimate and socially approved reasons to a wide range of illegal reasons.

Considerations of staying incognito are understandable for instance in the context of charity acts or for sheltering a person from unwanted contacting or persecution (Solove 2007, p. 139). Insofar, the possibility to act anonymously enables people among others to be more courageous with regard to their expression of opinions. Beyond that anonymous acting opens the chance to be heard free of prejudice or even offers an "identity thief" the opportunity to be heard at all. Not only in the information and communication sector anonymity plays a role; for example in a broader economic context, the French term for the US/UK "stock corporation" is "société anonyme", i.e. the shareholders of the corporation are not known since ownership should not be made known to the public; the participation is evidenced by bearer shares.

The movie "Anonymous" directed by Roland Emmerich and shown to the public in cinemas at the end of 2011 revisits this topic by seizing the conspiracy theory of William Shakespeare not being the originator of his published writings, thus referring to the aforementioned case configuration of pseudonymity. This theory's proponents, the so-called Oxfordians,[2] among others Mark Twain, Henry James and even Sigmund Freud, argue that William Shakespeare who came from a poor background did not possess the education for composing his writings, especially since he was rumored to be an analphabet. According to them, the actor William Shakespeare of Stratford, who has never been on foreign travel, could not possess such a special knowledge to historically correctly write the world-famous tragedies and comedies, as for instance "Henry V", "Othello" or "The Merchant of Venice".

To a great extent, these skeptics were of the opinion that Edward de Vere, the 17th Earl of Oxford, had been the true originator of the writings being published under the name of William Shakespeare. Edward de Vere, a culturally educated man who lived in Venice, Italy, for a while, was told to be a connoisseur of the Elizabethan court culture and a poet. The question of whether William Shakespeare himself or someone else was the originator of the writings published

---

[1] "Persecuted groups and sects from time to time throughout history have been able to criticize oppressive practices and laws either anonymously or not at all.": Talley v. California, 362 U.S. 60 (1960).

[2] Oxfordians are the supporters of the Oxfordian theory of Shakespearean authorship whereby Edward de Vere, 17th Earl of Oxford (1550–1604), wrote the writings traditionally attributed to William Shakespeare.

under the name of William Shakespeare divided the minds for centuries into Stratfordians[3] and Oxfordians even though to date there is no evidence for the defamatory statement of William Shakespeare not being the author of the writings attributed to him (exemplary: Sammartino 1990).

Even though there is a wide range of "good" reasons to stay incognito, the negative aspect of acting without being recognized is not to be underestimated since anonymity places people in the position to act much more unbiased and quite often meaner and less civiled in their speech (Solove 2007, p. 140) which involves the risk to harm other people's reputation. Simultaneously, staying anonymous by taking up another person's identity offers people the possibility of dodging behind a foreign identity and therewith grants the advantage of giving an opinion without bearing possible consequences on one's own behalf.

With the emergence and development of the online world the Internet became a valuable tool in everyday life encompassing social, cultural, economic and legal facets. Associated therewith the communications behavior of people all over the world has also changed; therefore, the particularities of the communication in the offline and the online world, particularly the anonymous communication, are to be addressed subsequently.

1.3 Characteristics of Communication

1.3.1 Real World

The term "real world" describes the "material, physical, atomic and molecular world of everyday human interactions" (Kabay 1998, p. 4). Forms of communication in the real world that indicate a disconnected state like talking on the telephone, writing letters or even talking face to face are referred to as communication in an "offline" world (Weber 2012a).

Communication within the offline/real world is characterized by anonymity (at least to a far extent) (Bizer 2000, pp. 61/62); neither paying a bill in a restaurant or supermarket in cash nor walking in public requires a previous complete announcement of the own identity. Briefly, at first glance the actors' identity is of minor importance within the real world.

Nevertheless, circumstances are different, if the aforementioned payment does not take place by cash but by a financial transaction through electronic payment mechanisms such as money or credit cards (Bizer 2000, p. 62). Within areas like these commercial relations or within personal matters the complete and veritable announcement of a person's identity is regarded as being of importance to guarantee a proper course of the respective procedure. The knowledge of the actors'

[3] Stratfordians are of the opinion that the actor William Shakespeare wrote all the works attributed to him.

identity is of fundamental importance since in case of business relations, assuming the buyer of a good pays with an ec-card, the buyer "just" promises the payment towards the seller. Insofar, the seller can prove a legitimate interest in the real identity of his business partner to protect him financially.

1.3.2 Particularities of the Online World

In addition to the long-known and omnipresent real world a parallel "environment", the so called virtual/online world (Internet), emerged within the last 30 years. In the course of the Internet's development and the increasing public acceptance communication to a great extent shifted into the virtual world and accordingly the issue of acting anonymously emerged there again.

1.3.2.1 Development of the Online World

Dating back to the late 1960s when U.S. researchers first developed protocols that allowed the sending and receiving of messages by use of computers,[4] the term "online" world was coined, referring to communicating via networked computers (Warschauer 2008, p. 207). In the course of the development and the spread of personal computers from the 1980s onwards communication via the Internet, online communication, started to become available to the public at large. Therewith, the percentage of people having Internet access and using web-based systems for the search and purchase of products or the cultivation of contacts has grown vastly since civil society has begun to replace traditional face-to-face communication by using e-services (Van Dijk et al. 2007, p. 7).

By now, working without Internet access is almost inconceivable, at least in developed countries. Rather, the medium Internet became so important for the societal communication that the participation of all is a substantial political task (Holznagel and Schumacher 2011, p. 14). Hence, the question arises of how to maintain all the benefits of the Internet while restricting antisocial communication and acting on the Internet (Kabay 1998, p. 2).

Being originally developed beyond a regulatory legal framework and mainly based on self-regulation by its users, initially the assumption prevailed that cyberspace was an independent new "province" and a legal vacuum in the world (Weber 2009, pp. 3–5 for further details). Thereby and with regard to the fact, that the Internet started as a communication platform of a comparatively small research and academic community (Weber and Schneider 2009, p. 18), the participants' identification within the World Wide Web played a minor role.

[4] The text of this subchapter is partly based on Weber 2012a.

In the course of time, the Internet established itself in everyday life (Demut and Rieke 2000, p. 38). Therewith, especially in view of to the developing electronic commerce, the participants' identifiability and traceability became of concern; just like within the offline world all parties to a contract have a clear interest in knowing their counterpart and obtaining information as for instance about solvency or credibility of further trade partners before concluding agreements.

However, as set out above, there is an interest of a wide range of (Internet) participants to partially stay incognito or even untraceable on the Internet, be it to prevent identity theft, to protect search histories from public disclosure, to get access to all websites or to avoid criminal prosecution.[5] Beyond the legal motivations some Internet users also seek for anonymously acting online to conduct fraudulent financial transactions or launch attacks with little risk of being located by law enforcement agencies and therewith aim at avoiding the consequences of a preceded or scheduled engagement in criminal or socially unacceptable behaviour. With commenters being given the possibility to hide behind a cloak of anonymity, the blog and Internet fora have become places for hatred, discrimination and bile (Adams 2011). Accordingly, the advantages and disadvantages of anonymous acting apply to both, anonymity in the real world ("offline") and in cyberspace ("online").

1.3.2.2 Surveillance and Identification of Internet Participants

(1) Subscriber Identification without the Internet Users' Knowledge

(a) Data Tracks

During the last twenty years Internet participants developed new ways for making use of the World Wide Web; thereby, it has become common practice to use the Internet for both retrieving and providing information (Taddicken 2012, p. 255). In order to be present on the Internet for private or professional purposes, an individual or an enterprise needs to have a specific address, an Internet Protocol (IP) address.[6] IP addresses are not physical and not directly controllable by the

[5] A relevant example in connection with anonymous acting online is the whistle-blowing Internet platform Wikileaks providing capacity for anonymously publishing submissions of private, secret, and classified media thereby following their goal of bringing "important news and information to the public" (http://wikileaks.org/About.html). Having released a number of significant documents in the past the entity sees itself as assistance to peoples of all countries who wish to reveal unethical behaviour in their governments and institutions.

[6] The Internet uses IP addresses to identify computers. Their addresses and names (then called host names) were initially stored on a centralized and monolithic file maintained by the Stanford Research International Network Information Center (SRI-NIC) on their NIC name server. By 1984, these addresses had become very complicated to use. That led people to translate these numbers into words and to organize them in the generic domains by the Domain Name System (DNS); for further details see Weber and Schneider 2009, pp. 19–21.

user since the allocation is (directly or indirectly) derived from Internet Address Registries.

The pool of IP addresses is managed by the Internet Assigned Numbers Authority (IANA),[7] which has since the early 1990s delegated the allocation of Internet resources to five established Regional Internet Registries (RIR) (Edelmann 2009, p. 3; Brunst 2009, pp. 51–53) that are obliged to take due regard to global addressing policies (Lehr et al. 2008, p. 9).[8] These non-profit RIR corporations[9] oversee the allocation of IP addresses to Internet Service Providers (ISP), National Internet Registries (NIR) and individual network institutions; these organisations in turn allocate IP addresses to the individual Internet users. Comparable to a piece of land in the real world, the establishment of a domain name traces out a "territory in cyberspace" which enables communication. To function properly IP address blocks can only be used by one network so as not to lead to conflicts in routing.

Many Internet users still believe in the anonymity of the Internet and the protection of their personal data as long as they do not disclose their identity by entering their name, private address or banking information (Pfitzmann 2000, p. 12; Solove and Schwartz 2011, p. 590; Schwartz and Solove 2011, p. 1837). This assumption is supported by the possibility to send emails or postal messages to electronic bulletin boards under pseudonyms (Solove and Schwartz 2011, p. 590).

In contrast, while surfing on the Internet every computer communicates by using a traceable IP address[10] and therewith leaves a data track on each passed website, meaning the website visited (Solove 2007, p. 147; Landau 2010, p. 139); website log files contain the user's IP address, the time he/she was online and any information the user entered into a webpage or pages the user downloaded (Solove and Schwartz 2011, p. 590). Beyond that, also each mobile phone or other device

[7] In 1989, the US Department of Commerce concluded a contract with the Department of Post and Telecommunications' Information Science Institute at the University of Southern California, establishing the Internet Assigned Numbers Association (IANA). Although IANA's tasks were transferred to a great extent to the Internet Corporation for Assigned Names and Numbers (ICANN), IANA among other things is still responsible for the global coordination of the Internet Protocol addressing system allocating IP addresses from the pools of unallocated addresses to the Regional Internet Registries (RIR) according to their needs; for further details see Weber and Heinrich 2011, pp. 78–80.

[8] At the beginning of the Internet, a single authority combined both service areas and distributed the information through the RFC series.

[9] At the present time there are five RIRs in operation, namely the American Registry for Internet Numbers (ARIN) for North America and Parts of the Caribbean, the RIPE Network Coordination Centre (RIPE NCC) for Europe, the Middle East and Central Asia, the Asia–Pacific Network Information Centre (APNIC) for Asia and the Pacific region, the Latin American and Caribbean Internet Addresses Registry (LACNIC) for Latin America and Parts of the Caribbean Region and the African Network Information Centre (AfriNIC) for Africa.

[10] That is why Internet users intending to visit a company webpage will mostly be redirected to the respective country page although having entered another top-level domain; businesses use this automatic onward transfer for selling products in different countries at different prices.

used to access the Internet has a unique IP address and can therewith potentially be traced (European Parliament 2010, p. 42). Accordingly, Internet Service Provider (ISP) (and any eavesdropper on the Internet connection) can monitor the steps users made on the Internet[11]; beyond that ISP have information to link an Internet user's screen name[12] with his/her real identity (Solove and Schwartz 2011, p. 591).

(b) Cookies and Other Applications

Each time the user visits a website also "Internet cookies" are downloaded into the user's electronic device tagging the user with an identification number; these identification numbers can include references to a wealth of information about the user (Solove and Schwartz 2011, p. 590). Internet cookies are small pieces of information in text format that are downloaded to the computer when the user visits a website (European Parliament 2010, p. 43). They may come from the page itself or from the providers of the advertising banners or other graphics that make up a website (Moore 2011, p. 233) and enable computers to remember a user's history on a particular website (Shah and Kesan 2004, pp. 13–17).[13]

A further possibility to identify Internet users by collecting information about them are so-called "web bugs". This technical device also known as "clear graphics interchange format (GIF)" (Nichols 2001, p. 1) is a graphic on a web page or inserted into an email created for the purpose of online tracking. The web bug enables the creator to determine who is reading a web page or email, when, how often, and from what computer. After the recipient opens the email the graphic shall be downloaded from the server eventually at least providing information about the used computer's IP address and the time of the request (Brunst 2009, p. 78). Initially developed in order to enable service providers to tailor services to meet Internet users' needs, the fact of people not recognizing this hidden monitoring makes these programs that dangerous since the tools can be used to monitor Internet users in case of legal and illegal activities (European Parliament 2010, p. 43).

(2) Self-imposed Subscriber Identification

In addition to the automatic collection of data many Internet participants still act very carelessly in dealing with the Internet and the protection of their own privacy. Even though they ascribe high importance to privacy (Barnes 2006), a large percentage of the user community is willing to share personal information under certain circumstances and frequently makes personal information available to third

---

[11] The announcement of the IP address is essential for enabling their locating by the respective web page operator and for knowing where to "send" the requested information to.

[12] The pseudonym he/she is appearing with on the Internet.

[13] "Cookies" are strings of data introduced by the company Netscape whereby the name was a term already in use in computer science for describing a piece of data held by an intermediary.

parties or allows them to store their personal or non-personal data. This careless behaviour with private data has the potential to lead to privacy and surveillance problems since a user's identity can be achieved by analyzing a "trail of seemingly anonymous and homogenous data left across different locations" (Malin et al. 2003, p. 1).

Several studies have shown that Internet participants in principle provide personal information on websites after request. As already outlined by a 2000 study, 54% of the polled Internet users have chosen to disclose personal information for using a website and an additional 10% would be willing to do this under the right circumstances; only a fourth of the persons asked would never provide personal information (Fox 2000, p. 2).

Furthermore, the dissemination of personal data is actively pursued by the constantly rising frequentation of social networks like Facebook or Myspace[14] and the therein offered possibility to present and position personal information by publishing pictures or giving details about the own private and professional life. According to a 2010 study by Ofcom, the government-approved regulatory authority for the broadcasting and telecommunication industries in the United Kingdom, 33% of the interviewees love putting private photos online, rising to 57% of those aged 16–24 (Ofcom 2010, p. 3). Even though 74% of the interviewed Europeans see disclosing personal information as an increasing part of modern life, only 26% of social network users feel in complete control of their personal data (European Commission 2011b, pp. 2, 22).

This acting very often enables or at least simplifies the Internet participant's identification. Even though the information disclosed should be available to the respective (identifiable) party only, the confidentiality or further transfer of these announced personal data is no longer subject to control by the respective Internet user.

Besides these aspects, with the progress of technical development the growing importance of Internet search engines contributes to the dissemination of data. Once online available data have been indexed by search engines, they can hardly be removed anymore from the World Wide Web. Hence, with the increased tendency to make information of all kinds public, privacy is at risk. Bearing in mind that the online world seems to be full of people willing to share personal information with others it may be easy to forget that there are many users who want to remain anonymous on the Internet (Glater 2006), especially as 70% of Europeans are concerned that their personal data held by enterprises may be used for purposes other than agreed at the time of collection (European Commission 2011b, p. 2).

[14] Social structures such as social networking sites, blogs and wikis made up for individuals (or organisations) that offer possibilities for participation and collaboration.

References

Adams T (2011) How the Internet created an age of rage. The Guardian. 24 July 2011. http://www.guardian.co.uk/technology/2011/jul/24/internet-anonymity-trolling-tim-adams. Accessed 31 Jan 2012

Barnes SB (2006) A privacy paradox: Social Networking in the United States. First Monday 11(9). http://firstmonday.org/htbin/cgiwrap/bin/ojs/index.php/fm/article/view/1394/1312. Accessed 31 Jan 2012

Bizer J (2000) Recht auf Anonymität—ein Rechtsprinzip der elektronischen Individualkommunikation, In: Sokol B (ed) Datenschutz und Anonymität. Toennes Satz + Druck GmbH, Düsseldorf. https://www.ldi.nrw.de/mainmenu_Service/submenu_Tagungsbaende/Inhalt/2000_Datenschutz_und_Anonymitaet/Datenschutz_und_Anonymitaet.pdf. Accessed 31 Jan 2012

Brunst PW (2009) Anonymität im Internet—rechtliche und tatsächliche Rahmenbedingungen. Duncker and Humblot, Berlin

Bundesamt für Sicherheit in der Informationstechnik (2001) Das Ende der Anonymität? Datenspuren in modernen Netzen. https://www.bsi.bund.de/ContentBSI/Publikationen/Studien/anonym/wasistanonymitaet.html;jsessionid=97B15124E289CE809BB8CA90471E5F9A.2_cid241. Accessed 31 Jan 2012

Demut T, Rieke A (2000) Der Rewebber—Anonymität im World Wide Web. In: Sokol B (ed) Datenschutz und Anonymität. Toennes Satz + Druck GmbH, Düsseldorf

Edelmann, B (2009) Running out of numbers: scarcity of ip addresses and what to do about it. Working Paper Harvard Business School. http://www.hbs.edu/research/pdf/09-091.pdf. Accessed 31 Jan 2012

European Commission (2011b) Special eurobarometer 359: attitudes on data protection and electronic identity in the European union. Report. June 2011. http://ec.europa.eu/public_opinion/archives/ebs/ebs_359_en.pdf. Accessed 31 Jan 2012

European Parliament (2010) Information and communication technologies and human rights. http://www.europarl.europa.eu/committees/en/studiesdownload.html?languageDocument=EN&file=31731. Accessed 31 Jan 2012

Fox S (2000) Trust and privacy online: why americans want to rewrite the rules. The Pew Internet and American Life Project. http://www.pewinternet.org/~/media//Files/Reports/2000/PIP_Trust_Privacy_Report.pdf.pdf. Accessed 31 Jan 2012

Froomkin AM (1995) Anonymity and Its enmities. Journal of Online Law. http://articles.umlaw.net/froomkin/Anonymity_Enmities.htm. Accessed 31 Jan 2012

Glater JD (2006) Privacy for People Who Don't Show Their Navels. The New York Times. 26 January 2006. http://www.nytimes.com/2006/01/25/technology/techspecial2/25privacy.html. Accessed 31 Jan 2012

Holznagel B, Schumacher P (2011) Die Freiheit der Internetdienste. In: Kleinwächter W (ed) Grundrecht Internetfreiheit. Eurocaribe Druck Hamburg, Berlin

Kabay ME (1998) Anonymity and pseudonymity in cyberspace: deindividuation, incivility and lawlessness versus freedom and privacy. http://www.mekabay.com/overviews/anonpseudo.pdf. Accessed 31 Jan 2012

Landau S (2010) Surveillance or Security? The risks posed by new wiretapping technologies. The MIT Press, Cambridge and London

Lehr W, Vest T, Lear E (2008) Running on empty: the challenge of managing Internet addresses. http://cfp.mit.edu/publications/CFP_Papers/Lehr%20Lear%20Vest%20TPRC08%20Internet%20Address%20Running%20on%20Empty.pdf. Accessed 31 Jan 2012

Malin B, Sweeney L, Newton E (2003) Trail re-identification: learning who you are from where you have been. LIDAP-WP12. Carnegie Mellon University. Laboratory for International Data Privacy. http://dataprivacylab.org/dataprivacy/projects/trails/paper3.pdf. Accessed 31 Jan 2012

Moore R (2011) Cybercrime: investigating high-technology computer crime, 2nd edn. Anderson Publishing, Burlington

Nichols S (2001) Big Brother is Watching: An update on web bugs. http://www.sans.org/reading_room/whitepapers/threats/big-brother-watching-update-web-bugs_445. Accessed 31 Jan 2012

Ofcom (2010) Media Literacy Matters, Online trust and privacy: People's attitudes and behaviour. Research Document. http://stakeholders.ofcom.org.uk/binaries/research/media-literacy/trust-privacy.pdf. Accessed 31 Jan 2012

Pfitzmann A (2000) Möglichkeiten und Grenzen von Anonymität. In: Sokol B (ed) Datenschutz und Anonymität. Toennes Satz + Druck GmbH, Düsseldorf

Sammartino P (1990) The man who was William Shakespeare. Cornwall Books, New York

Schwartz PM, Solove DJ (2011) The PII problem: privacy and a new concept of personally identifiable information. New York Univ Law Rev 86(6):1814–1894

Shah RC, Kesan JP (2004) Recipes for cookies: how institutions shape communication technologies. http://www.governingwithcode.org/journal_articles/pdf/Recipe_For_Cookies.pdf. Accessed 31 Jan 2012

Solove DJ (2007) The future of reputation: gossip, rumor, and privacy on the internet. Yale University Press, New Haven

Solove DJ, Schwartz PM (2011) Information Privacy Law, 4th edn. Wolters Kluwer Law, New York

Taddicken M (2012) Privacy, surveillance, and self-disclosure in the social web: exploring the user's perspective via focus groups. In: Fuchs C, Boersma K, Albrechtslund A, Sandoval M (eds) Internet and Surveillance: The Challenges of Web 2.0 and Social Media. Routledge, New York

Van Dijk G, Minocha S, Laing A (2007) Consumer, channels and communication: online and offline communication in serve consumption. Interact Comput 19:7–19

Wallace KA (1999) Anonymity. Ethics Inf Technol 1(1):23–35

Warschauer M (2008) Online communication. In: Carter R, Nunan D (eds) The Cambridge guide to teaching english to speakers of other languages. Cambridge University Press, Cambridge

Weber RH (2009) Internet governance: regulatory challenges. Schulthess, Zurich

Weber RH (2012a) International governance in a new media environment. In: Price ME, Verhulst SA (eds) Handbook of media law and policy: a socio-legal exploration. Routledge, New York (forthcoming)

Weber RH, Heinrich UI (2011) IP Address allocation through the lenses of public goods and scarce resources theories. scripted 8(1): 69–92. http://www.law.ed.ac.uk/ahrc/script-ed/vol8-1/weber.pdf. Accessed 31 Jan 2012

Weber RH, Schneider T (2009) Internet governance and Switzerland's particular role in its processes. Schulthess, Zurich

Chapter 2
Anonymity Challenges in the Internet

Since information about people acting in the Internet (both, consciously or unconsciously provided by them) can be easily found, surfing on the World Wide Web is far from an anonymous activity of no consequences. With regard to the therewith associated risk of data abuses it is still a debatable point, whether the identification in the online world is essential, and if so to what extent, or whether there is a right to act anonymously within the World Wide Web.

In this sense, light will subsequently be shed on the motivations for the anonymous use of Internet services and the Internet participants' possibilities to make their activities on the Internet untraceable.

2.1 Risks for Anonymous Use of Internet Services

Manifold Internet activities cause risks for those persons being interested to remain anonymous when using the new communication channels and platforms. Some practices leading to data collection and consequently to the possibility of third persons to have access to personal data are discussed hereinafter.

2.1.1 Information Gathered by IP Addresses

Internet IP addresses[1] are used to route data from one host computer to another. Even though these numerical addresses do not directly identify particular Internet users, their identification can easily follow from the connected addresses by evaluating the gathered information (Schwartz and Solove 2011, pp. 1838/1839).

Initially, static IP addresses were used. A static IP address is a number (in the form of a dotted quad) that is assigned to a computer by an Internet Service

[1] See Sect. 1.3.2.2(1)(a).

R. H. Weber and U. I. Heinrich, *Anonymization*, SpringerBriefs in Cybersecurity,
DOI: 10.1007/978-1-4471-4066-5_2, © The Author(s) 2012

Provider (ISP) to be its permanent address. Accordingly, with each log on to Internet access the user is allocated the same IP address (Freund and Schnabel 2011, p. 496). In the end, this facilitates the tracing of the respective computer and therewith the identification of the Internet participant.

At the time of the Internet's inception, scarcity of IP address space seemed to be unlikely as information and communication technologies (ICT) were cost-intensive and therefore only few networks were interested in Internet connections (Edelmann 2009, pp. 1–13). In the course of the last 15 years the demand for IP addresses has enormously increased. Eventually, since IPv4 makes only available about four billion IP addresses, the exhaustion of the current Internet Protocol addressing system, Internet Protocol Version 4 (IPv4), occurred in February 2011.

Already more than ten years ago (in 1998) the substitute for IPv4, namely IPv6, was designed, aiming at providing quantitative and qualitative advantages compared to IPv4, the two Internet Protocols are currently not fully compatible (Weber and Heinrich 2011, p. 71). The problem of shortage could be mitigated by various techniques such as "Network Address Translation" (NAT) (Brunst 2009, p. 52), which hides multiple Internet hosts behind a single IP address by connecting private networks to the public Internet. However, such a procedure would have the disadvantage of breaking end-to-end connectivity. As a result, Internet activity would no longer be fully granted, making it difficult to establish Internet telephone calls directly between two hosts using standard Voice over Internet Protocols (VoIP) (Weber and Heinrich 2011, pp. 70/71). Furthermore, the method would increase complexity since there are two classes of computers (some with public and some with private addresses) as well as costs for design and maintenance of networks and for the development of applications (European Commission 2008).

Hence, with regard to the temporary scarcity of IP addresses and their associated sparing use, dynamic IP addresses were allocated by the Regional Internet Registries (RIRs) to the respective access providers which enable the access to the Internet and therewith serve as an interface between user and Internet; access provider administrate a small pool of IP addresses and allocate these addresses for the period of usage only (Brunst 2009, p. 51). Subsequently, a further allocation to a "new" user connecting to the Internet is possible. With regard to the impermanent allocation of IP addresses an exact tracing of the respective user is difficult and requires a recording at the material time; otherwise each of the access authorized computers could potentially have done the respective action (Brunst 2009, p. 51).

Since even Internet participation by using dynamic IP addresses is not qualified to preclude the respective Internet user's tracing with absolute certainty,[2] achieving the possibility of surfing on the Internet without revealing one's IP address and therewith the own identity must be seen as the most effective method to realize anonymity.

---

[2] Complete anonymity cannot be guaranteed.

2.1.2 Storage of Recorded Data

Although being partly (as far as scope and duration of storage is concerned) illegal according to most current national law (Freund and Schnabel 2011, p. 496)[3] many providers storage recorded data over a long period of time (Krause 2003, p. 161). In reality, data like the time of visit of a website, the used Internet IP address and the whole history of surfing are collected. The web page operators' prior intention to collect all these data usually is to conduct marketing analyses for streamlining their webpages and therewith increasing their business opportunities.

Furthermore, web page operators collect data for the protection of their own web page against misuse. Even if most of the individual data collected are insufficient to support a conclusion on the respective user the sum of data may have the ability to identify the user or his computer, respectively (Malin et al. 2003, p. 1); accordingly, the storage of data possesses a threat to anonymity. The period of time of data storage must (also) be put in relation with the right to be forgotten encompassing the right to have data deleted after a certain period of time.[4]

2.1.3 Insufficient Data Security Measures

With the development of new technologies, new attacking tools are also regularly developed. Therefore, security is and has to remain a topic of discussion. Since security and privacy of data are of particular importance for Internet participants both private and business, transactions and the interests of all parties involved have to be kept confidential in order to protect the Internet participants' privacy and ensure fair competition.

The online world is rich in possibilities; technical innovations and ingenuity allow the society to progress and prosper. However, the development of new forms of technical activity can also potentially be misused, among others by measures like denial of service attacks, dissemination of viruses, logical bombs or hacking (Weber 2009, p. 232):

- *Denial of service attacks* (DoS) consist of large streams of useless data directed towards particular network locations with the aim of overloading equipment and destroying its functionality. A denial-of-service attack does not steal passwords or manipulate data, but rather overloads the data traffic of certain systems (flood attack) or causes parts of the system's hardware or software to shut down.

[3] Example: According to German law, access providers are only allowed to use stored data for accounting purposes or for eliminating technical barriers.

[4] Extensively on the subject of Trojan horses, see Sect. 4.4.

In so-called distributed denial-of-service attacks (DDoS) multiple systems flood the bandwidth or resources of a targeted system.
- A *virus* is a program that can copy itself, and is therefore attached to or inserted in data documents or the boot sector of the hard disk. A virus is often capable of deleting data or of invalidating certain functions of computer software or the download of further Trojan horses.[5] Recently, attackers often bundle link virus programs with other malicious programs making viruses a major threat to private users and businesses (Graham et al. 2011, p. 92).
- Programs that are attached to any other program and lead to the shutdown of the system are called *logical bombs*.
- The most serious technical attack is arguably the actual *hacking* into a communication system; the term "hacking" is often used for a broad range of illegal objectives and technical activities.

During the past view years, experience has shown that hackers and attackers are breaking into vital portions of the global network infrastructure, causing problems and creating costs (Weber 2003, p. 105 ss). This was the scenario on December 24, 2011, when hackers using the pseudonym "Anonymous",[6] accessed to the database of Stratfor, a global security intelligence firm, and copied customer data like email addresses and credit card data. The goal of this action was to steal altogether one million dollar for gifting the money as Christmas donations to aid agencies.[7] Similarly, a group of people announcing to use the pseudonym "Anonymous" threatened to block certain servers or deviate some information flows if the US Congress would approve the pending proposal for a "Stop Online Piracy Act" (SOPA) in late January 2012

Within the last few years repeatedly individuals or groups of people using the alias "Anonymous" appeared on the Internet accomplishing hacker attacks. In so doing, among others in June 2011 "Anonymous" temporarily incapacitated the online presence of GEMA, a German collecting society, for protesting against the GEMA's claims to remuneration towards the video portal YouTube which result in the fact that most of the music videos cannot be accessed.

---

[5] In more detail see Sect. 4.4.1.1.

[6] Starting in 2008, a group of online activists acting under the synonym "Anonymous" appeared on the scene. In so doing, the name "Anonymous" itself was inspired by the (perceived) anonymity under which Internet participants post images and comments on the Internet. Representing the concept of any and all people as an unnamed collective the members of the group appear in public wearing the Guy Fawkes masks popularized by the comic book and film V for Vendetta. At the beginning, "Anonymous" provided warnings against the Church of Scientology and accomplished protest actions to support the right to freedom of speech and the Internet freedom. Initially acting only within the Internet, the activist meanwhile expanded their protest actions in sectors aside from the Internet. The activists sign their messages with "We are Anonymous. We are Legion. We do not forgive. We do not forget. Expect us."

[7] With regard to the fact that on behalf of "Anonymous" both a letter claiming responsibility and a denial was sent the perpetration of "Anonymous" is still unproved. According to the denial letter of December 25, 2011, "Anonymous" strongly condemned the action of being a violence of the freedom of press.

Regardless of the acting entity's intentions these and further incidents stress the relevance of data security in connection with the Internet. The actions have shown that a threat—for example, the shut down or attempt to shut down major sites used by an entire community to accomplish essential civil tasks—can go beyond a simple menace to economic safety and endanger national and international security. An umbrella term for such threats to infrastructure is "cyberterrorism", which is defined as an "extreme or intense force in an online setting, causing unexpected or unnatural results, and used for purposes of intimidating, coercing, or creating an atmosphere of anarchy, disorder, or chaos in a networked environment" (Biegel 2001, p. 232).[8]

In view of the wide difference between anonymous and untraceable acting (Solove 2007, p. 147; Schwartz and Solove 2011, p. 1837), as few as possible traces should be left in order to accomplish the aforementioned Internet users scope to achieve data protection and data security (Köhntopp 2000, p. 44). Hence, anonymizing services (also referred to as anonymizers) come into operation for masking the own IP address meanwhile surfing on the World Wide Web and therewith holding out the prospect of achieving data security and for realizing unobserved movements in the World Wide Web.

2.2 Technical Implementation of Anonymizing Services

Even though it is relatively easy to surf on the Internet without immediately revealing one's identity or to blog anonymously on the Internet, it is hard to be untraceable, too. With regard to the previously described informative content of IP addresses individuals can (more or less easily) be followed without them even knowing about it (Weber and Weber 2010, p. 45). Accordingly, in recent years the wish for anonymous communication on the Internet has motivated the development of a number of networking techniques.

2.2.1 Privacy Enhancing Technologies in General

Technological measures are available that increase privacy in the application layer. A number of technologies have been developed in order to achieve information privacy goals.[9] Privacy Enhancing Technologies (PET) can be oriented on the subject, the object, the transaction or the system. Subject-oriented PET aim at limiting the ability of other users to discern the identity of a particular business, object-oriented PET endeavour to protect identities through the use of particular

[8] In general to the problems of cyberterrorism see Council of Europe (2008).

[9] This subchapter is based on Weber and Weber 2010, pp. 47–50.

technology, transaction-oriented PET have the goal to protect transactional data through e.g. automated systems for destroying such data, and system-oriented PET want to create zones of interactions where users are hidden and objects bear no traces of businesses handling them nor records of interaction (Samuelson 2000, p. 1668; Froomkin 2000, pp. 1528–1553).

A further category is being developed by the World Wide Web Consortium (W3C) and is called a Platform for Privacy Preferences (P3P). P3P is supposed to enable individuals to program their browsers to identify which information they are willing and unwilling to disclose to the owners of the website (Samuelson 2000, p. 1668). This server-based filtering tool allows for identification and protection against deviations from the applicable codes of conduct in the privacy field (Weber 2009, p. 245).

2.2.2 Anonymizing Networking Techniques

In case encryption is not used almost all data retrieved by an Internet participant can be intercepted and seen by others. Insofar, as already said, the avoidance of collection of individual-related data best protects the informational and communicative self-determination of the persons concerned (Holznagel and Sonntag 2000, p. 72).

Applied by both Internet users (client anonymity) and service providers (server anonymity) anonymizers are among others used to hide the user's true physical location (Graham et al. 2011, p. 75) towards providers and other Internet participants for preventing conclusions on the respective identity by automatically anonymizing the Internet traffic (Brunst 2009, p. 131).[10] In that sense, light will be shed on some of the developed, partially cost-free services to facilitate anonymous Internet access hereinafter.

2.2.2.1 Client Anonymity

(1) Simple Proxy Service

The most utilized technical and easy to handle devices used for veiling the own activities are web-based proxy servers, also known as web-based proxies. Serving as intermediary between user and target page, a proxy server is a computer that forwards requests by other computers. By allowing actors to send network traffic through another computer the sender's IP address transmission is hampered by the proxy server (Graham et al. 2011, p. 75).

[10] However, anonymizing services do not automatically anonymize the communication's content.

Instead of connecting directly to the webserver, Internet participants make a circuit and connect to the proxy server first; afterwards, the proxy server connects to the requested page (Brunst 2009, pp. 52/53). As a result, the targeted server gets information solely about the proxy server's IP. Since the transmission of the user's IP is prevented, from the target page's point of view the Internet user makes no appearance (Krause 2003, p. 161).

(2) Mix Cascades

Although staying incognito to the target page operator when using a simple proxy server the Internet participant does not remain really anonymous; the proxy server's operator has the ability to ascertain the used computer. With regard to the ultimate aim of Internet anonymization to allow a host to communicate with an arbitrary server to an effect that nobody can determine the host's identity, newly anonymizing services connect proxy server in series, so called mix cascades or multiple proxies (Krause 2003, pp. 161, 173/74).

These independent devices mingle the incoming bitstreams and direct them through a large number of computers whereby an exact allocation of the requesting Internet participant is prevented or at least hampered since none of the servers involved has all information at his disposal. The final receiver can only discover the last proxy and is not directly communicating to any of the intermediary proxies or the sender of the information respectively his computer (Graham et al. 2011, p. 75).

(3) Onion Routing

The main idea of onion routing is to encrypt and mix Internet traffic from many different sources whereby onion routing protects the identity of the sender and the receiver of data both towards third parties and from each other (Berghel and Womack 2003, p. 18). With onion routing, data is wrapped into multiple encryption layers, using the public keys of the onion routers on the transmission path. This process would impede matching a particular IP packet to a particular source. A well-known anonymization service implementing this technique is the free software TOR ("The Onion Router").[11]

(4) Peer-to-Peer (P2P) Systems

Differently to the services explained above, within peer-to-peer (P2P) systems all computers enjoy equal rights to the effect that they utilize and allocate services. While P2P systems in the beginning still relied on a central root, the most

---

[11] See https://www.torproject.org/; Landau (2010), p. 139/40.

advanced forms of P2P systems operate without a centralized server. Data as well as inquiries for information are decentralized, and each peer only has access to his/her own communication data (Weber and Weber 2010, p. 50).

According to this system all peers are potential originators of the respective traffic and are also potential relays. Being part of the net each "peer" makes information available. Since none of the peers governs the net no participant knows the complete amount of forwarded data but just the peers he/she is collaborating with (Brunst 2009, p. 68). If communication is encrypted, the system enjoys a high degree of anonymity as communication cannot be intercepted and search of data is carried out indirectly through chains (Mayrhofer and Plöcklinger 2006, pp. 11–15).

The interest in utilizing P2P system has increased over the course of time, based on the wish to share files without revealing one's network identity and risking litigation, the distrust in governments and the increasing number of lawsuits against bloggers. The most common P2P type of use is the peer-to-peer filesharing application, in recent years frequently used for the illegal sharing of soundfiles and cinematic works protected by copyright. Besides, there are also legal grounds of justification for using peer-to-peer filesharing applications, as for instance the protection of free speech.

(5) Crowds

A further anonymizing technique is called "crowds". In contrast to the above described proxies that forward request by other computers, *crowds* work by hiding the actual source of data sent by an Internet user by "burying" it in the traffic of a "crowd" of users. Accordingly, each member of the crowd could be the sender of the received Internet traffic. Since this technique uses a just a single symmetric key there is less encryption necessary and data traffic can be forwarded faster (Brunst 2009, pp. 135–137).

2.2.2.2 Server Anonymity

As set out above, the most promising way to achieve data security and data protection is to mask or replace the own IP address. In certain cases not only the user of Internet services but also the service provider wishes to remain anonymous especially with regard to the fact that individuals often act as servers when participating in file sharing networks or hosting personal web pages (Bono et al. 2004, p. 1). The arguments given above regarding client anonymity are applicable on server anonymity, too. A service provider can also have an interest in staying incognito, as for instance in case a public interest group aims at publishing without taking on the risk of becoming subject to repressive measures (Demut and Rieke 2000, p. 40).

2.2.3 *Virtue of Anonymizing Services*

Anonymizing services are employed to accomplish the goal of achieving data security and therewith maintaining the power of control over the own data. Basically, anonymizers themselves and their use are not illegal (Graham et al. 2011, p. 78) even though the use to conduct an illegal activity is not allowed. Therefore, most anonymizing services provide rules within their general business terms, among others obliging the user to omit occurrences of illegal activity. As a consequence, infringements of the business terms may result in information exchanges between service providers and investigative authorities.[12]

In terms of efficiency of anonymizing services some critical annotations need to be made. Basically, proxy servers, mix cascades, onion routing, P2P systems and crowds have the ability to meet the envisaged goal.

With regard to possible technical failures or abuses the interposition of just one proxy server, however, involves the risk of missing the intended anonymity. Hence, the usage of mix cascades is preferable since these chains of proxy servers mingle the incoming bitstreams, direct them through a large number of computers and therewith to a great extent prevent the requesting Internet participant's IP address identification. However, since the encrypted bitstreams at the first and the last proxy remain without encryption, this kind of partial encryption cannot offer an adequate protection towards an observing attacker. Furthermore, the utilization of series-connected proxy servers noticeably decelerates the data stream.

Even though onion routing protects the identity of both the sender and receiver of data, this technique negatively affects the Object Naming Service (ONS)[13] and discovery services by increasing time of waiting and thereby resulting in performance issues. Furthermore, onion routing could only be used for the anonymization of traffic directed at EPCIS servers, thereby increasing anonymity, but not confidentiality or integrity of data.

Within regard to P2P systems, anonymity is not always given. Contrary to the general opinion of ordinary file-sharing applications being able to ensure anonymity, there is at most anonymity between the file-sharer and other users, but not necessarily vis-à-vis law enforcement agencies (Brunst 2009, p. 98). Only within anonymous P2P networks might it be possible to remain undetected by state control (Brunst 2009, pp. 98, 102).

Within a crowd the data traffic is routed through a great number of users thereby at first glance obliterating all traces (Berghel and Womack 2003, p. 18). Since there is no single server forwarding requests to receivers, every participant of the crowd could be the forwarder of traffic. However, this technical device's weak point consists of the fact that also the forwarder's IP address will be transmitted

---

[12] Compare for example Anonymizer, Terms of Use, http://www.anonymizer.com/legal/legal, Accessed 12 January 2012.

[13] The ONS is a service containing the network addresses of services; for further details see Weber and Weber 2010, p. 6.

which in case of investigative measures would lead to the computer having accepted the request at last before forwarding the requested data to the receiver (Brunst 2009, p. 137).

In a nutshell, it can be said that the use of anonymizing services is adapted for fulfilling the individuals' need to make an appearance on the Internet without revealing his/her identity even though complete anonymity seems to be a wishful thinking. However, it is debatable whether the advantages offered by such anonymizing services[14] do outweigh the disadvantages (Baeriswyl 2008, p. 4). Taking this assessment into account, subsequently the possible legal bases for the right to act anonymously on the Internet and therewith the use of (Internet) anonymization services are to be addressed.

References

Baeriswyl B (2008) Der Schatten über der Anonymität. Digma 1:4–5

Berghel H, Womack K (2003) Anonymizing the net: sanitizing packets for fun and profit. Communications of the ACM 46(4): 15–20. http://delivery.acm.org/10.1145/650000/641220/p15-berghel.pdf?ip=130.60.119.66&acc=ACTIVE%20SERVICE&CFID=62809855&CFTOKEN=52124798&__acm__=1327076953_549d640167b855013cd4ba7bd5ac87e2. Accessed 31 Jan 2012

Biegel S (2001) Beyond our control?: confronting the limits of our legal system in the age of cyberspace. MIT press, Cambridge

Bono SC, Soghoian CA, Monrose F (2004) Mantis: a lightweight, server-anonymity preserving, searchable P2P network. http://files.dubfire.net/jhu/publications/mantis-tr-b.pdf. Accessed 31 Jan 2012

Brunst PW (2009) Anonymität im Internet—rechtliche und tatsächliche Rahmenbedingungen. Duncker and Humblot, Berlin

Council of Europe (2008) Cyberterrorism: the use of the internet for terrorist purposes. Council of Europe Publishing, Strasbourg

Demut T, Rieke A (2000) Der Rewebber—Anonymität im World Wide Web. In: Sokol B (ed) Datenschutz und Anonymität. Toennes Satz + Druck GmbH, Düsseldorf

Edelmann, B (2009) Running out of numbers: scarcity of ip addresses and what to do about it. Working Paper Harvard Business School. http://www.hbs.edu/research/pdf/09-091.pdf. Accessed 31 Jan 2012

European Commission (2008) Communication from the Commission to the European Parliament, the Council, the Economic and Social Committee and the Committee of the Regions: Advancing the Internet: Action plan for the deployment Internet Protocol version 6 (IPv6) in Europe. COM 2008(313). 27 May 2008. http://ec.europa.eu/information_society/policy/ipv6/docs/european_day/communication_final_27052008_en.pdf. Accessed 31 Jan 2012

Freund B, Schnabel C (2011) Bedeutet IPv6 das ende der anonymität im internet? MultiMedia und Recht 8:495–499

Froomkin AM (2000) The death of privacy? Stanford Law Rev 52:1461–1543

[14] During the so called "Jasmin Revolution" starting at the end of 2010 in Tunesia and continuing 2011 within the bordering Arab States governments (unsuccessfully) tried to silence the political opposition by shutting down important webpages. However, by using anonymizing services Internet users were able to bend this censorship of the Internet.

Graham J, Howard R, Olson R (eds) (2011) Cyber security essentials. Auerbach Publications, Boca Raton

Holznagel B, Sonntag M (2000) Rechtliche anforderungen an anonymisierungsdienste: das beispiel des janus-projektes der fernuniversität hagen. In: Sokol B (ed) Datenschutz und Anonymität. Toennes Satz + Druck GmbH, Düsseldorf

Köhntopp M (2000) Identitätsmanagement—anforderungen aus nutzersicht. In: Sokol B (ed) Datenschutz und anonymität. Toennes Satz + Druck GmbH, Düsseldorf

Krause C (2003) Tools für anonymität. In: Bäumler H, von Mutius A (eds) Anonymität im internet. Vieweg, Braunschweig

Landau S (2010) Surveillance or Security? The risks posed by new wiretapping technologies. The MIT Press, Cambridge and London

Malin B, Sweeney L, Newton E (2003) Trail re-identification: learning who you are from where you have been. LIDAP-WP12. Carnegie Mellon University. Laboratory for International Data Privacy. http://dataprivacylab.org/dataprivacy/projects/trails/paper3.pdf. Accessed 31 Jan 2012

Mayrhofer M, Plöcklinger O (2006) Aktuelles zum internetrecht: tagungsband zum symposium internet-recht vom 23. April 2005. Pro Libris, Engerwitzdorf

Samuelson P (2000) Privacy as intellectual property? Stanford Law Rev 52:1125–1173

Schwartz PM, Solove DJ (2011) The PII problem: privacy and a new concept of personally identifiable information. New York Univ Law Rev 86(6):1814–1894

Solove DJ (2007) The future of reputation: gossip, rumor, and privacy on the internet. Yale University Press, New Haven

Weber RH (2003) Towards a legal framework for the information society. Schulthess, Zurich

Weber RH (2009) Internet governance: regulatory challenges. Schulthess, Zurich

Weber RH, Heinrich UI (2011) IP Address allocation through the lenses of public goods and scarce resources theories. scripted 8(1): 69–92. http://www.law.ed.ac.uk/ahrc/script-ed/vol8-1/weber.pdf. Accessed 31 Jan 2012

Weber RH, Weber R (2010) Internet of things: legal perspectives. Schulthess, Zurich

Chapter 3
Legal Foundations of Anonymity

Even though the individuals' motivations of operating anonymously on the Internet are manifold, their highest common denominator is the protection of (the own) privacy. Although everyone takes privacy in normal life for granted, trying to get the same level of privacy and anonymity on the Internet are as important as it is difficult to achieve the objective (Martin 2006). In so doing, the netizens' privacy in the online world needs to be defended against both the States (for example, under security interests) as well as against private actors, in terms of economic or criminal interests (Benedek 2008, p. 40).

The law of the Internet is characterized by international and supranational regulations. Hereinafter, light will be shed on the assessment of whether these regulations contain provisions regarding the protection of anonymous acting on the Internet. With this in mind, human rights frameworks as well as specific legislative acts will be addressed.

3.1 International Legal Framework

To date, an international legal framework generally covering anonymity does not exist. With regard to the aforementioned close interrelation between anonymity and privacy, regulations referring to privacy may contain applicable provisions.[1]

An internationally binding agreement generally covering privacy does not (yet) exist and the many facets of personal information would also make it very difficult to find a reasonable common denominator in the varying legal systems; subse-

[1] Privacy as a human right is enshrined in many international legal instruments, for example in Article 12 of the Universal Declaration of Human Rights (UDHR) (United Nations 1948), in Article 17 of the International Covenant on Civil and Political Rights (ICCPR) (United Nations 1966) as well as in Article 8 of the European Convention for the Protection of Human Rights and Fundamental Freedoms (ECHR) (Council of Europe 1950). Some key aspects of these international legal instruments are to be described subsequently.

R. H. Weber and U. I. Heinrich, *Anonymization*, SpringerBriefs in Cybersecurity,
DOI: 10.1007/978-1-4471-4066-5_3, © The Author(s) 2012

quently the international and supranational regulations are looked at closely with regard to the question whether they contain regulations having the potential to provide the basis for a right to act anonymously on the Internet.

Furthermore, anonymization also relates to data retention as since the early days of implementation of data protection laws the issue of data storage has played a certain role. Data protection has to deal with the collection and the processing of data; but even if these activities are done in a legally compliant way, the question remains whether data should not be destroyed after a certain time period in view of an individual's interest to keep certain information undisclosed from a given moment onwards.

During the last few years, the issue of data retention has become a more intensively discussed topic, especially in light of the terrorist attacks, for example in New York, London and Madrid. Consequently, lawmakers and law enforcement authorities were eager to pass laws which oblige private companies to compulsorily store data, especially communication data, such as mobile-phone data or email-data, to be used in criminal investigations. Such laws entail, however, several substantial critical topics: Besides the costs thereby imposed on private companies due to the compliance with said rules the scope of data protection remains a debatable theme. It is obvious that law enforcement authorities need to have access to communication data in order to work effectively.[2] Nevertheless, it is crucial that the fundamental right of data protection is not undermined, because it is one of the cornerstones constituting the rule of law. Therefore, a data retention policy must balance legal and privacy concerns against public and/or economic needs by evaluating aspects such as the retention time, archival rules, data formats, and the permissible means of storage, access, and encryption.

Hereinafter, light will be shed on the regulations[3] issued by the United Nations, the Organisation for Economic Co-operation and Development, the Council of Europe and the European Union as examples for international privacy protection frameworks.

3.1.1 United Nations

3.1.1.1 Universal Declaration of Human Rights and the International Covenant on Civil and Political Rights

The term "anonymity" is not explicitly mentioned in the Universal Declaration of Human Rights (UDHR) (United Nations 1948). However, Article 12 of the UDHR deals with privacy, stating that "no one shall be subjected to arbitrary interference with his privacy, family, home or correspondence, nor to attacks upon his honour

---

[2] See Chap. 4.

[3] This list is not intended to be exhaustive.

and reputation" and that "everyone has the right to the protection of the law against such interference or attacks".

As the UDHR, the International Covenant on Civil and Political Rights (ICCPR) (United Nations 1966) also contains no specific regulations addressing arrangements for acting on the Internet anonymously by making use of anonymizing services. Nevertheless, Article 17 ICCPR enshrines the protection of privacy, literally repeating the wording of Article 12 UDHR and emphasizes that interferences with privacy must not be unlawful.

Insofar, with regard to the correlation of privacy and anonymity, a right to stay anonymous on the Internet can be (indirectly) deduced from these regulations. Nevertheless, the problem of any constitutional provision consists in the fact that the protection is directed towards the realization of a human right and less towards a justified allocation of information and non-information. Moreover, looking at the historical background, the constitutional provisions have not been designed with a view to the particular needs of the digital society since the provisions were negotiated and debated prior to the implementation of the Internet.

3.1.1.2 Guidelines for the Regulation of Computerized Personal Data Files

In 1990, the UN General Assembly adopted Guidelines for the Regulation of Computerized Personal Data Files (United Nations 1990). This step taken by the UN emphasised the importance of data protection not only in the industrialized countries, but also in the whole global community. However, it cannot be overlooked that the UN Guidelines are recommendations to national legislators and international organisations, not legal norms being binding upon them or even the private enterprises or citizens (United Nations 1990: introduction).

The guidelines do not contain any regulation regarding the anonymous use of the Internet. Concerning data retention, the UN Guidelines state in Principle 3 lit. c that the storage of personal data may not exceed the period of time which is necessary for the achievement of the purpose they were stored for. But the issue of data retention remains a marginal topic; it is merely determined that stored data still must serve a purpose. The UN Guidelines do, apart from the mentioned principle, not state under which conditions and during what period of time certain personal data may be stored. The UN has also not made any attempts to refine the rules regarding data retention in the recent past. Furthermore, for the time being, there are no efforts that would lead to a change of the rules in the near future.

The UN Guidelines for the Regulation of Computerized Personal Data Files are not suitable for the justification of a right to anonymity on the Internet; they rather address the handling of computerized personal data files and therewith presuppose the collection of data which in turn contradicts a right to act anonymously on the Internet without leaving data traces.

3.1.2 OECD

Furthermore, the OECD Guidelines on the Protection of Privacy and Transborder Flows of Personal Data of 1980 (OECD 1980), an important international economy-oriented legal instrument, might have the potential to protect the right to act anonymously on the Internet.

Although not legally binding on OECD Member States, these recommendations can serve as minimum standards for the legislation of the Member States (OECD 1980, part four). For reputational reasons, the Member States of the OECD are required to take into account the contents of the Guidelines and subsequent interpretations in the legislative process (Weber 2002, p. 155).

While the 1980 Recommendations established an internationally highly esteemed minimum standard of data protection, they do not offer any legal framework for data retention. The explanatory memorandum (OECD 1980, explanatory memorandum, No. 54), however, states with respect to para. 9 of the 1980 Recommendations, that stored data which do not longer serve any justifiable purpose should be deleted, since the lack of interest in them may lead to loss of or negligence with such data and hence poses a threat to privacy. This early statement marked an important step in international data protection rule-making since it was acknowledged that the permanent storage of data beyond their utility might result in an infringement of data privacy.

The OECD since then published numerous other Guidelines in the data protection field, the most important being the Guidelines for the Security of Information Systems (OECD 2002).

The OECD Recommendations and Guidelines do not offer any legal framework for substantiating a right to act anonymously on the Internet; comparable with the UN Guidelines for the Regulation of Computerized Personal Data Files, however, the general direction of improving the protection of individuals against a misuse of data might indirectly contribute to anonymity.

3.1.3 Council of Europe

3.1.3.1 European Convention on Human Rights

Having been signed in Rome on November 4, 1950, the European Convention for the Protection of Human Rights and Fundamental Freedoms (ECHR), released by the Council of Europe, sets forth a number of fundamental rights and freedoms (Council of Europe 1950: summary). Containing both substantive and procedural rights, the ECHR does not explicitly mention the word “anonymity” or the protection of anonymous actions at all. In view of the close relation of anonymity to privacy and free speech (Akdeniz 2002, p. 224), however, an assessment of the importance of Articles 8 and 10 ECHR in this context is worth to be done hereinafter (Trenkelbach 2005, p. 143).[4]

(1) Privacy Protection

Awarding everyone the right to have his private and family life, his home and his correspondence respected, Article 8 para 1 ECHR aims at protecting privacy as a whole (Gollwitzer 2005, Article 8, margin number 1).

The term "private life" encompasses both, the inner circle as well as the relationships to other people (Brunst 2009, p. 286). Therewith, also the right to remain anonymous to others and actions like identification checks and monitoring measures are affected. Therefore, the right to use anonymizers to enforce anonymity within the World Wide Web can be traced back to Article 8 ECHR.

The legally protected good "home" describes a physical place where personal life or family life may unfold (Weber and Sommerhalder 2007, pp. 57/8 with further references). The protection of the home serves the security of the people and the individual's well-being, accordingly, interferences with the legally protected good must be based on a legal foundation.

The term "correspondence" clearly includes materials which cross by post; additionally, the European Court of Human Rights also included communication by telephone[5] and by pager. With regard to the fact that by now vast amounts of personal data are transferred and exchanged online,[6] also communication sent by emails is encompassed.[7] Hence, with regard to the debate about the existence of a right to act anonymous on the Internet, in this context, online surveillance[8] of Internet participants' correspondence is of major concern. In light of the term's broad interpretation, all forms of information addressed to one or several addressees and the information's transmission are comprised starting at the information output up to the transport and the receipt in the end. Hence, the lag or hindrance of the correspondence's delivery constitutes an interference of Article 8 ECHR (Weber and Sommerhalder 2007, p. 57).

---

4 Concerning the area of tension between the Articles 8 and 10 ECHR see in general Weber and Sommerhalder 2007.

5 See European Court of Human Rights (ECHR): Klass and others vs. Germany. judgment of 6 September 1978. Series A No. 28, para 41.

6 According to a 2011 Survey of the European Commission 94% of the Europeans aged 15–24 are using the Internet, see European Commission 2011b, p. 4.

7 See ECHR: Copland vs. The United Kingdom, judgment of 3 April 2007, No. 62617/00, para 42.

8 Online surveillances enable investigators to look at all data stored on the suspect's computer (correspondence by email, pictures, documents) unknown to him/her and therewith affects the suspect's legal position to a great extent since the obtained information's content can be enormous. As in the case of eavesdropping a suspect's Internet telephony, online surveillances are accomplished with the aid of (later explained) Trojan horse software and require an explicit warrant.

Indeed, in certain case configurations injuries are allowed, provided they concern one of the goals out of Article 8 para 2 ECHR, are essential within a democratic society and are proportional (Wildhaber and Breitenmoser 1992, margin number 525).[9]

(2) Freedom of Expression

A further component to the right to anonymity and therewith the right to use anonymizers can be deduced from the right to freedom of expression (Article 10 ECHR), entitling everybody the "freedom to hold opinions and to receive and impart information and ideas without interference by public authority" (Article 10 para 1 sentence 2), since anonymity can be essential to free speech (Solove 2007, p. 139). With regard to the interrelation between anonymity and privacy the tensions between the freedom of expression and the right to privacy must be examined more closely.

Information privacy contradicts freedom of expression and speech, meaning the free marketplace of ideas, since privacy stops people from speaking about others.[10] Restrictions of the freedom of expression can be contractually agreed (within certain limits) or be linked to intellectual property rights. If, moreover, privacy is considered as a general restriction of a fundamental freedom of speech, not only would its scope be substantially narrowed,[11] but this approach might also become a problematic prejudice for additional limitations of this basic freedom.[12] Therefore, the different constitutional values need to be carefully weighted.

Since anonymity can be essential to free speech (Solove 2007, p. 139) an adequate protection of the freedom of expression needs to include the anonymous expression of opinions as being absolutely guaranteed. Hence, Article 10 ECHR can be consulted to substantiate the right to connect to the Internet anonymously by using anonymizing services (Trenkelbach 2005, pp. 146/47). Taking the opposite view, at least this effect can be entitled by additionally consulting Article 8 ECHR (Brunst 2009, p. 298).

---

[9] As to that, the European Court of Human Rights emphasizes the necessity of an effective control against abuse; Pätzold 2012, Article 8 para 126.

[10] In this sense Volokh 2000, p. 1049; on the corresponding inherent conflict also Grewlich 1999, pp. 270, 272.

[11] For more details Volokh 2000, pp. 1057 ss, 1073 ss.

[12] This major concern, expressed by Volokh throughout his extensive study, requires careful attention (particularly Volokh 2000, pp. 1076/77, 1122/23).

3.1.3.2 Automatic Processing of Personal Data

Furthermore, the Convention No. 108 for the Protection of Individuals with regard to Automatic Processing of Personal Data (Council of Europe 1981) needs to be mentioned, being the first binding international instrument protecting the individual against abuses which may accompany the collection and processing of personal data.[13]

The Convention extended the safeguards to cover everyone's right to have his/her privacy respected and right to keep certain information confidential, taking account of the increasing cross-border flow of personal data undergoing automatic processing. Participating parties are required to take the necessary steps in their national legislation for guaranteeing respect in their territory for the privacy rights of all individuals with regard to processing of personal data.

The term anonymity is not explicitly mentioned in the Convention of 1981; solely, Article 7 of the Convention addresses data security, stating that "appropriate measures shall be taken for the protection of personal data stored in automated data files against accidental or unauthorized destruction or accidental loss as well as against unauthorized access, alteration or dissemination". Dealing with already stored data, this regulation is not suitable for sufficiently substantiating a right to act anonymously on the Internet.

Article 11 (Extended protection), stating that „none of the provisions of this chapter shall be interpreted as limiting or otherwise affecting the possibility for a Party to grant data subjects a wider measure of protection than that stipulated in this convention", could be sufficient to reflect a right to anonymity; this, however, could eventually be considered as being contrary to the Convention's underlying principle of automatic processing of data.

3.1.4 European Union

3.1.4.1 EU Fundamental Rights Charter

The legally non-binding Charter of Fundamental Rights of the European Union (European Parliament 2000), based, in particular, on the fundamental rights and freedoms recognised by the European Convention on Human Rights, contains similar regulations.

Like the ECHR the Fundamental Rights Charter does also not explicitly mention the term "anonymity". Nevertheless, repeating the wording of Article 8 para 1 ECHR, Article 7 of the Fundamental Rights Charter equally aims at protecting the individual's privacy. Highlighting the fact that according to Article 52 para 3 Fundamental Rights Charter the scope of the rights guaranteed therein

[13] Summary of the treaty: http://conventions.coe.int/Treaty/en/Summaries/Html/108.htm.

corresponds to the rights guaranteed by the ECHR, also Article 7 Fundamental Rights Charter is adapted to provide the basis for a right to remain anonymous to others and therewith the right to use anonymizing services on the Internet.

Furthermore, Article 8 para 1 Fundamental Rights Charter, granting everyone the right to the protection of his own personal data,[14] can be consulted for the derivation of a right to use Internet anonymizers since the most successful way to achieve data security on the Internet is to remain anonymous by hiding or replacing the own IP address.

3.1.4.2 EU Privacy Policies

In addition, the European privacy policies forming the statutory framework for the protection of personal data might also have the potential to protect the right to act anonymously on the Internet.

(1) Data Protection Directive and Directive on Privacy and Electronic Communications

After the pioneer work done by the UN, the OECD and the Council of Europe,[15] the EU fielded a complex and comprehensive Directive on the Protection of Individuals with Regard to the Processing of Personal Data and on Free Movement of such Data (Data Protection Directive) in an effort to harmonize and improve national data protection laws (European Parliament 1995). This step sets a milestone in the protection of personal data. Later on, the European Data Protection Directive was complemented in light of recent technological developments by the Directive Concerning the Processing of Personal Data and the Protection of Privacy in the Electronic Communications Sector (Directive on Privacy and Electronic Communications) (European Parliament 2002).

As far as anonymity is concerned, Recital 26 as well as Article 6 para 1 lit. e Data Protection Directive and Recital 9 as well as Articles 6 and 9 of the Directive

[14] As in Article 16 of the Treaty of the European Union stating that "everybody has the right to the protection of personal data concerning them"; http://eur-lex.europa.eu/LexUriServ/LexUriServ.do?uri=OJ:C:2008:115:0047:0199:EN:PDF.

[15] With a very few exceptions is was not until the second half of the 20th century that governments in Europe started establishing data protection laws encompassing also the issue of data retention. In 1968, at a time when the world could not yet anticipate the technological progress and its effects on data retention, the Council of Europe released a Recommendation concerning human rights and modern scientific and technological developments. Already at that time this Recommendation recognized the potential risks for individual rights. Later, in 1981, the Council of Europe released a Convention for the Protection of Individuals with regard to Automatic Processing of Personal Data (No. 108). Since then, the Committee of Ministers of the Council of Europe released several Recommendations entailing additional provisions which refine the notion of data retention.

on Privacy and Electronic Communications need to be looked at closely from the point of view whether the Directives are adapted to find arguments regarding the creation of a right to act anonymously on the Internet.

Pursuant to Recital 26 of the Directive 95/46/EC "the principles of protection must apply to any information concerning an identified or identifiable person" provided "either by the controller or by any other person" an identification of the said person may be done. Additionally, Article 6 para 1 lit.e Data Protection Directive states that personal data "must kept in a form which permits identification of data subjects for no longer than is necessary for the purposes for which the data were collected or for which they are further processed".

Recital 9 of the later enacted Directive 2002/58/EC highlights the "objective of minimising the processing of personal data and of using anonymous or pseudonymous data where possible", supplemented by the instruction to erase or anonymize no longer needed traffic data (Article 6), and the request to anonymize location data of users or subscribers (Article 9). In detail, Article 6 para 1 codifies that "traffic data [...] must be erased or made anonymous when it is no longer needed for the purpose of the transmission of a communication".

Even though both Directives contain regulations regarding anonymity at large, it is a debatable point whether these regulations are sufficient to reflect a right to act anonymously/use anonymization on the Internet.

The Data Protection Directive refers to a subsequent anonymization of already transferred and no longer needed traffic data. Generally speaking, there is no argument for having the right to act anonymously on the Internet. In contrast, the Directive on Privacy and Electronic Communications explicitly mentions the use of anonymous data which might be interpreted as a right to act anonymously on the Internet (by using anonymizers).

Sixteen years after its release the main principles and the objectives of the Data Protection Directive still remain relevant. However, the rapid technological developments make it necessary to modernise the notion of data protection in the 21st century. Therefore in 2010, the European Commission published a Communication on Personal Data Protection in the European Union (European Commission 2010) addressing newly arisen challenges and stating that one of the goals[16] of the new legislative action in the area of data protection should be the clarification of the recently much discussed (and below explained) right to be forgotten.[17]

Encompassing the right of an individual to demand that his/her data will be deleted as soon as such data is no longer needed for legitimate reasons, in the

---

16 According to a recently published press release of the European Commission, the "goals were to protect individuals' data in all policy areas, including law enforcement, while reducing red tape for business and guaranteeing the free circulation of data within the EU" (European Commission 2012a).

17 Extensively on the subject Sect. 3.2.2.3.

case of a data storage for which consent is required and if this consent is withdrawn, the data in question must be deleted.[18]

Besides the right to be forgotten, several other points to enhance the individuals' control over their data are proposed by the Commission. In order to exercise control over personal data, it is crucial that modalities for access, identification and ultimately deletion are improved. For example, such modalities would encompass provisions to access personal data electronically or the introduction of deadlines for answering to requests concerning stored data. Furthermore, due to the rising importance of social networks and other services or applications which permanently store personal data, sometimes without the possibility of deletion, the Commission suggests introducing provisions ensuring the portability of such data. Those provisions would enable individuals to withdraw their data from such services without being obstructed by the data controller. All these proposals aim at strengthening the protection of privacy by expanding the individuals' control over their stored data.

After a first draft version of the review of the Data Protection Directive of 1995 surfaced in December 2011,[19] on January 25, 2012, the European Commission published its proposal regarding a comprehensive reform of the EU's data protection rules of 1995, among others aiming at strengthening online privacy rights and therewith helping reinforce Internet user confidence in online services (European Commission 2012a) by (1) improving the individuals' ability to control their data (encompassing the above mentioned right to be forgotten), (2) improving the means for individuals to exercise their rights, (3) reinforcing data security and (4) enhancing the accountability of those processing data (European Commission 2012b, pp. 6/7). The European Commission's proposal encompasses both a proposal for a Directive (European Commission 2012d) and a proposal for a regulation (European Commission 2012c).

With regard to the ongoing debates about the existence or justification of a right to act anonymously on the Internet the implementation of the proposed comprehensive reform might create more clarification for the future (particularly with regard to the mentioned right to be forgotten), since making data retention impossible is the most effective way of data security.

(2) European Data Retention Directive

Despite the prevalent notion of data retention that data should no longer be stored or should be made anonymous after its purpose had expired, the EU deemed it

[18] For a comprehensive approach on personal data protection in the EU see European Commission 2010, p. 8.

[19] In the last quarter of 2011, the European Commission maintained intensive dialogues with Europe's national data protection authorities and with the European Data Protection Supervisor to investigate options for more consistent application of EU data protection rules across all EU Member States, see European Commission 2012b, p. 3.

necessary to establish a framework requesting from providers of electronic communication services to store customers' traffic and location data and allowing law enforcement authorities to access said data. Already during the law-making process, the legislative basis for the Directive was heavily debated. Discussions have taken place whether it could be based on the first Pillar of the EU, the power of the Union relating to the single market, or on the Third Pillar, the legislative powers in the field of police and judicial cooperation in criminal matters. Ultimately, it was decided to base the Directive on the First Pillar, since it seemed the best avenue in view of the fact that the fundamental right of data protection would be affected (Bignami 2007, p. 239 ss).

The European Data Retention Directive was passed by the EU Parliament and the Council on March 15, 2006 and subsequently published on April 13, 2006, in the Official Journal of the Union (European Parliament 2006). Thereupon Ireland brought a claim before the Court of Justice of the European Union (ECJ) arguing that the Directive should have been based on the legislative powers of the European Union within the Third Pillar and not on the competence of the EU in the single market and would therefore be invalid. The ECJ, however, considered the legislative basis of the Directive, in particular Article 95 of the Treaty on the Functioning of the European Union (European Union 2010), as sufficient and dismissed the case (Court of Justice of the European Union 2009). Notwithstanding this decision, the question whether the fundamental right of data protection is adequately protected remains to be assessed.

One of the primary goals of the Directive is to enable law enforcement authorities and intelligence agencies to access stored communication, traffic and location data, thereby improving criminal investigations. Consequently, providers of electronic communications' services are obliged to retain traffic and location data, which might be used to identify the registered user. Pursuant to Article 6 of the Directive such data should be retained at least six months, but in any case not longer than two years. The data in question include fixed network and mobile phone traffic and location data as well as Internet and email connection and traffic data; the content of the communication, such as the transcript of a conversation or the text of an email, is, however, not to be retained (European Parliament 2006, Article 5 para 2). According to the Directive the data retained might be available for the purpose of investigation, detection and prosecution. But the Data Retention Directive does not define the kind of crimes or threats that would allow the respective authorities to access the stored data, nor does it require the Member States to define them. Besides the partly unclear language of the Data Retention Directive, the burden on the providers to fulfil the requirements is substantial, especially the incurred costs for the collection of data and storage and the uncertainty of reimbursement by national governments.

The Directive has set the deadline for the comprehensive implementation of its provisions into national law at the latest by 15 March 2009. However, some Member States, such as Germany, Romania and the Czech-Republic, have failed to yet correctly implement the Directive into national law.

After Germany had transposed the required provisions into national law in 2007 (Deutscher Bundestag 2007), this law was partly rendered invalid[20] by the German Federal Constitutional Court,[21] ruling that data retention generates a perception of surveillance which would impair the free exercise of fundamental rights; the keeping of some kind of personal information may be a violation of Article 8 European Convention on Human Rights (Council of Europe 1950).

The Court deemed the German regulations regarding data retention unconstitutional and disproportionate. According to the Court, the mentioned regulations lack detailed security measures, clearly stated applications as well as legal protection and transparency rules, especially in view of the fact that the law in question would allow the production of highly sensitive personality and mobility profiles of a major part of the population (De Simone 2010, p. 314).

Even though data retention for strictly limited use situations along with sufficiently high security measures for data does not necessarily violate the German Basic Law, the Constitutional Court emphasizes that the retention of such data constitutes a serious restriction of the right to privacy and therefore shall only be admissible under particularly limited circumstances. As to that, a retention period of six months should be the upper limit of what could be considered proportionate (German Federal Constitutional Court 2010, para 215). Furthermore, data shall only be requested in cases of already existing suspicions of serious criminal offences or evidences of a risk to public security and shall be encoded with transparent supervision of their use (European Commission 2011a).

In June 2011, the German government has presented a new draft for the implementation of the Directive but as Germany has failed to transport the Directive into national law within the specified time limit, the country now faces proceedings before the Court of Justice of the European Union for not fulfilling its contractual duties. The Constitutional Courts of Romania and the Czech-Republic have also declared the respective national data protections laws unconstitutional, bringing forward the argument that the Directive's implementation would infringe the protection of privacy as well as the right to information self-determination.[22]

Moreover, it is uncertain whether a collection of communication data retained by the Internet Service Providers (ISP) really proves to be very effective, since users increasingly tend to move their communication for example into discussion

---

[20] In December 2010, the Working Group on Data Retention—a citizens' movement—brought an action with 35.000 complainants before the German Federal Constitutional Court demanding amongst other things additional guarantees for the freedom of electronic communication, limitations and cutbacks of existing surveillance powers and a restraint on the introduction of such new powers; see De Simone 2010, p. 306 ss.

[21] After the German Federal Court issued an (again extended) injunction in 2008, prohibiting law enforcement authorities the access to retained data, the Court nullified the German Data Retention Law on March 2, 2010, 1 BvR 256/08.

[22] Romania: Decision no. 1258 of 8 October 2009, published in: Official Gazette no.798 of November 23, 2009; Czech Republic: Data Retention in Telecommunications Services, 2011/03/22–Pl. ÚS 24/10.

fora, social networks or even virtual environments such as online role playing games rather than using email services (Brown 2010, p. 97 ss). Furthermore, popular peer-to-peer communications, such as Skype, are also not monitored by traditional ISP (Brown 2010, p. 98).

Summarizing, the European Data Retention Directive does not seem to be really sufficient to reflect a right to use anonymizers for acting anonymously on the Internet since the Directive aims at storing traffic data for a certain period of time and therewith aims at detecting Internet participants instead of protecting their privacy.

3.2 Concretization of the Human Rights Protection Regime

Since anonymity and privacy on the Internet are very important even if they are still difficult to achieve (Martin 2006), in the following the importance of the above outlined human right on privacy and its impact on a (potential) right on anonymity will be discussed in more detail.

3.2.1 Correlations of Anonymity and Privacy

Information technology has fundamentally changed society and communication has become much easier and faster with the advent of the Internet (Weber 2012b, p. 273). Such change brings uncertainty with it, in particular because directing, controlling, and enforcing traditional norms has become more difficult, even if risks to privacy in the digital environment were sounded some time ago (presaged in George Orwell's 1984).[23]

Hence, the protection of personal data (on the Internet) must be considered a key issue, in particular in realizing the right to privacy. Data protection should become an essential guarantee for balancing the interests related to privacy (individual freedoms and security requirements) against the wish for information exchange in the public interest (Council of Europe 2002).

The term "privacy" conveys a large number of concepts and ideas.[24] In this respect, three basic features of privacy should be considered, namely (1) secrecy, i.e. information known about an individual, (2) solitude, e.g. access to an individual and finally (3) anonymity, i.e. attention paid to an individual (Wacks 2000, p. 238; Weber 2009, p. 237). Anonymity as a particular aspect of privacy has to do with autonomy, namely the individual choice of not disclosing the name when

[23] See Orwell 1949.

[24] Warren and Brandeis 1890, p. 205 (refer to the right "to be let alone"); Hosein 2006, pp. 122–125 and 131–135.

communicating by way of the Internet. Seen from this angle, privacy in the form of anonymity can be described as the freedom to control one's own information (Cheung 2009, p. 209; Weber, 2012b, p. 281). Following this concept, this kind of autonomy is "about maintaining informational privacy, controlling dissemination and disclosure of information about ourselves, and protecting ourselves against unwanted access by other people" (Cheung 2009, p. 210).

Consequently, privacy allows keeping certain information and data confidential (Weber 2009, p. 240) and is therewith supported by anonymity describing a condition of being unknown or unacknowledged to others.[25] Insofar, anonymity and privacy have certain similarities since "protection" is an important issue for both. Nevertheless, extensive privacy (achieved by anonymity) might cause problems in case of criminal behaviour of the concerned person and could even lead to an evasion of accountability for harm done to others.

3.2.2 Protection Regime of Privacy

3.2.2.1 Scope of the Fundamental Right

Privacy is a fundamental but not an absolute right (European Parliament 2010, p. 42) aiming at the protection of an individual sphere free from national and international surveillance, encompassing a large number of concepts and ideas[26] and speaking of the part of every person's life in which personal autonomy may be impressed (Jackson 2011, para 21.055).

Privacy is not a value itself; moreover the decisive factor (the spatial issue) consists in the relationship between a person and an information (Weber 2002, p. 150). In particular, different kinds of data vary in relevance depending upon the person in question, because the importance or value of information relates to the given context in the information society (Reidenberg 2000, p. 1323; Posner 1998, p. 395).

In practical life, the most important objective of privacy is the prevention of improper use of personal information in whatever way (Kang 1998, 1214 ss). Therefore, individuals want to control access to their personal information; in complying with this objective, three areas related to privacy can be identified (Kang 1998, pp. 1202–1211):

- Physical space can be comprehended as a shield against unwanted objects or signals; in this sense privacy is close to infrastructure security.

---

[25] See Sect. 1.1.

[26] Privacy encompasses different legal aspects, an important foundation can be seen in the right of liberty and human dignity; for a recent overview see Cheung 2009, pp. 191–217; the text of this subchapter is partly based on Weber 2012b, pp. 273–280.

- Decision-making power may be required in relation to information flow: the objective here is the protection of a person's freedom to make self-defined choices in respect to data dissemination without State interference.
- Information privacy can be understood as an individual's control over processing: in this context the acquisition, disclosure, and use of personal information is at issue.

Personal information also plays a role in civil and criminal law; furthermore, the confidentiality of certain classified data is decisive both for governments and enterprises. For these reasons, it is not surprising that a coherent legal framework of privacy is nearly impossible to achieve. Nevertheless, the human right character of privacy remains the basis for its scope and contents, particularly since human rights provide for the only universally recognized system of values (Marzouki 2006, p. 197 ss).

3.2.2.2 Inherent Limits of Privacy

Obviously, human rights are not unlimited since the exercise of a human right by an individual can interfere with the parallel human right of another individual; insofar rights and freedoms are limited by the corresponding values of others (Weber 2002, p. 208). Furthermore, restrictions related to the exercise of human rights may also be imposed by the principle of morality or of public order as defined by the States: Each sovereign body wants to have some inalienable principles realized which are considered as minimum standards of those citizens living together (Benedek 2006, p. 23; Marzouki 2006, p. 198). Particularly, States are interested to avoid that individuals are misusing fundamental freedoms to the own benefit and to the detriment of others.

The described technical developments offer considerable advantages in terms of efficiency and productivity, but they also entail potential risks which are to be mirrored in the light of human rights' limits. Modern technologies provide near-term access to limitless quantities of personal data and establish the possibility of creating "personality profiles" through the combination of different data files (Council of Europe 2002, Sect. 17); this is facilitated by surveillance technology, potentially causing a considerable increase in individual privacy infringements (Benedek 2008, pp. 43–47).

The monitoring of all actions would result in a serious restriction of the individual's freedom of action (European Parliament 2010, pp. 42/43) even though security might call for data collection efforts, at least if surveillance is in the public interest. Certainly, the risk of governments abusing their power by justifying everything with the public interest is imminent, as shown using the example of the Chinese online instant messenger Tencent QQ[27] reportedly having recorded users'

[27] QQ is an international messenger with more than 1 billion registered and 500 million monthly active accounts and, according to their own statements, the most popular instant messaging service and the largest online community in China; see http://www.tencent.com/en-us/index.shtml.

online communication[28] and having delivered the reports to the police upon request (OpenNet Initiative 2009, p. 15).[29]

Control and access, however, can be looked at from two sides: On the one hand, holders of private information are interested in controlling it and (in case of third party control) accessing it; on the other hand, third persons might have a legitimate right to make information transparent. The conflicting interests must be balanced through an evaluation of the weight of the contradicting values.

As a consequence, the right to rely on anonymity cannot be without limits; interests of other persons and the general public interest must be taken into consideration. Thereby, the interest balancing test should be designed in way that the individual right is respected to the farthest possible extent, but not anymore if higher ranking public interests could be endangered.

3.2.2.3 Right to be Forgotten in Particular

The lately much discussed and already mentioned right to be forgotten might also be of relevance with regard to privacy and, correspondingly, to anonymity since the included "delete" process causes privacy to the farthest possible extent. Realizing that the Internet is never forgetting anything has led to the demand for a "right to be forgotten" as a new human right.[30] Such right to be forgotten must include the right of individuals to control the way in which their data is being used and aims at making certain information disappear after the lapse of a certain time period. In particular, individuals have to be able to deactivate their own tags.

Obviously, the interests of States may require the disclosure of certain information. For these reasons, a balance of interest test must be applied in conflicting situations (Weber 2011a, p. 122, no. 14). However, as mentioned, privacy or a right to keep personal information confidential could be in conflict with other rights, such as free speech and other privileges related to the free use of the web. Eventually, the question remains, whether the right to be forgotten actually is to be considered as "privacy" right since privacy concerns information that is not publicly known.

In 2010 a first legislative project was developed in France that envisaged the creation of a right to be forgotten in the World Wide Web (Charte du droit à l'oubli dans les sites collaboratifs et les moteurs de recherche 2010). Subsequently, not much concrete information was made available about the proposed law, which was intended to force online and mobile firms to dispose of emails and text messages after an agreed-upon length of time or at the request of the individual

[28] By installing a keyword blocking program (OpenNet Initiative 2009, p. 15).

[29] Unfortunately, this is not only a problem in countries with limited human rights protection; among others also Germany and the USA accomplished excessive citizen surveillance and monitoring (European Parliament 2010).

[30] Extensively on this subject Weber 2011a and Mayer-Schönberger 2009.

concerned. In November 2010, the EU Commission took up the idea of introducing a right to be forgotten (European Commission 2010)[31] in the context of the ongoing revision of the Data Protection Directive 95/46/EC.[32] The EU proposal focuses on a right that would allow an individual to have his or her data deleted. Eventually, in January 2012, the European Commission published a proposal on the protection of individuals with regard to the processing of personal data and on the free movement of such data (European Commission 2012c). This "fundamental reform of the EU's data protection framework" (European Commission 2012b, p. 3) encompasses the data subject's right to be forgotten and, for strengthening this right, the right to erasure (European Commission 2012c, Considerations 53, 54, Article 17).

As a consequence of this new kind of freedom, also called "silence of the chips" (Benhamou 2006, pp. 8, 9), certain information cannot anymore be activated and, therefore, becomes completely anonymous. The deactivation of tags is a technical measures leading to the same result as the acknowledgment of a legal right (to privacy). Being based on the right of the personality and encompassing several elements such as dignity, honour, and the right to private life, the right to be forgotten would make it possible to an individual to keep certain (past) things secret by making activity trails invisible. As a consequence, holders of information are relying on their own autonomy to individually decide on the possible use of their own data and, therefore, on the anonymization of information (Weber 2011a, p. 120 ss, no. 5).

To date, the outcome of the aforementioned legislative EU proposal is still uncertain even though the users' equipment with an effective right to be forgotten and to erase in the online environment (European Commission 2012c, Article 17) is somehow heavily pushed by the Commission. Otherwise, a further careless handling of own or foreign personal data could lead to the situation that there is hardly any personal information protected from the prying eyes and ears of the public/state.

3.2.2.4 Interim Assessment

Even though a review of the international legal framework has shown that the right to act anonymously on the Internet is not explicitly included in the available instruments so far, there is no evidence that a right to anonymity should be excluded from the protection regime since the closely related right on privacy being widely protected at the international level allows to draw conclusions on the issue of anonymity within the World Wide Web. Consequently, the right to act

[31] This approach has been repeatedly reiterated by members of the European Commission, for example by EU justice commissioner Viviane Reding in a speech to the European parliament on 16 March 2011.

[32] In more detail see Sect. 3.1.4.2(1).

anonymously can be at least indirectly based on international legal instruments even id the exact scope of protection seems to be rather vague.

Therefore, a right to act anonymously in the Internet can to some extent be deduced from the Universal Declaration on Human Rights, the OECD Guidelines on the Protection of Privacy and Transborder Flows of Personal Data, the European Convention on Human Rights, the Charter of Fundamental Rights of the European Union and the European Union's Data Protection Directive and Directive on Privacy and Electronic Communications. Additionally, the lately developed and soon to be implemented right to be forgotten might be invoked to justify a right to anonymous acting online.

References

Akdeniz Y (2002) Democracy and cyberspace. Social Res Int Q 69(1):223–237

Benedek W (ed) (2006) Understanding human rights: manual on human rights education. Berliner Wissenschafts-Verlag, Vienna

Benedek W (2008) Internet governance and human rights. In: Benedek W, Bauer V, Kettemann MC (eds) Internet governance and the information society: global perspectives and european dimensions. Eleven International Publishing, Utrecht

Benhamou B (2006) Organizing internet architecture. http://www.diplomatie.gouv.fr/en/IMG/pdf/Organizing_Internet_Architecture.pdf. Accessed 31 Jan 2012

Bignami FE (2007) Privacy and law enforcement in the european union: the data retention directive. Chicago J Int Law 8:233–255

Brown I (2010) Communications data retention in an evolving internet. Int J Law Inf Technol 19(2):95–109

Brunst PW (2009) Anonymität im Internet—rechtliche und tatsächliche Rahmenbedingungen. Duncker and Humblot, Berlin

Charte du droit à l'oubli dans les sites collaboratifs et les moteurs de recherche (2010). 13 Oct 2010. http://www.aidh.org/Actualite/Act_2010/Images/Charte_oubli_La_Charte.pdf. Accessed 31 Jan 2012

Cheung AS (2009) Rethinking public privacy in the internet: a study of virtual persecution by the internet crowd. J Media Law 1(2):191–217

Council of Europe (1950) European Convention for the Protection of Human Rights and Fundamental Freedoms. Summary. http://conventions.coe.int/Treaty/en/Summaries/Html/005.htm. Accessed 31 Jan 2012

Council of Europe (1981) Convention for the Protection of Individuals with regard to Automatic Processing of Personal Data. 28 Jan 1981. http://conventions.coe.int/Treaty/Commun/QueVoulezVous.asp?NT=108&CL=ENG. Accessed 31 Jan 2012

Council of Europe (2002) Contribution to the 2nd preparatory committee for the World Summit on Information Society: Democracy, Human Rights and the Rule of Law in the Information Society. 9 Dec 2002. http://www.itu.int/dms_pub/itu-s/md/03/wsispc2/c/S03-WSISPC2-C-0032!!PDF-E.pdf. Accessed 31 Jan 2012

Court of Justice of the European Union (2009) Judgement of the Court of 10 Feb 2009 (case C-301/06) (Ireland versus the European Parliament and the Council of the European Union). http://eur-lex.europa.eu/LexUriServ/LexUriServ.do?uri=CELEX:62006J0301:EN:NOT. Accessed 31 Jan 2012

De Simone C (2010) Pitting Karlsruhe Against Luxembourg? German Data Protection and the Contested Implementation of the EU Data Retention Directive. German Law J 11(3):291–318

Deutscher Bundestag (2007) Gesetz zur Neuregelung der Telekommunikationsüberwachung und anderer verdeckter Ermittlungsmassnahmen sowie zur Umsetzung der Richtlinie 2006/24/EG (Law on the Revision of Telecommunications Monitoring and other Covert Investigation Measures and on the Implementation of Directive 2006/24/EC). 21 December 2007. http://www.gesmat.bundesgerichtshof.de/gesetzesmaterialien/16_wp/telekueberw/telekueberw-index.htm. Accessed 31 Jan 2012

European Commission (2010) Communication from the Commission to the European Parliament, the Council, the Economic and Social Committee and the Committee of the Regions: A comprehensive approach on personal data protection in the European Union. COM(2010) 609 final. 4 Nov 2010. http://ec.europa.eu/justice/news/consulting_public/0006/com_2010_609_en.pdf. Accessed 31 Jan 2012

European Commission (2011) Report from the Commission to the Council and the European Parliament. Evaluation report on the Data Retention Directive (Directive 2006/24/EC). COM(2011) 225 final. 18 April 2011. http://www.cep.eu/fileadmin/user_upload/Kurzanalysen/Vorratsdatenspeicherung/COM_Data_Retention_Evaluation_en18042011.pdf. Accessed 31 Jan 2012

European Commission (2011b) Special Eurobarometer 359: Attitudes on Data Protection and Electronic Identity in the European Union. Report. June 2011. http://ec.europa.eu/public_opinion/archives/ebs/ebs_359_en.pdf. Accessed 31 Jan 2012

European Commission (2012a) Commission proposes a comprehensive reform of data protection rules to increase users' control of their data and to cut costs for businesses. Press release. 25 Jan 2012. http://europa.eu/rapid/pressReleasesAction.do?reference=IP/12/46&format=HTML&aged=0&language=EN&guiLanguage=en. Accessed 31 Jan 2012

European Commission (2012b) Communication from the European Parliament, the Council and the European Economic and Social Committee and the Committee of the Regions: Safeguarding Privacy in a Connected World. A European Data Protection Framework for the 21st Century. COM(2012) 9 final. 25 Jan 2012. http://ec.europa.eu/justice/data-protection/document/review2012/com_2012_9_en.pdf. Accessed 31 Jan 2012

European Commission (2012c) Proposal for a Regulation of the European Parliament and of the Council on the protection of individuals with regard to the processing of personal data and on the free movement of such data (General Data Protection Regulation). COM(2012) 11/4 draft. http://ec.europa.eu/justice/data-protection/document/review2012/com_2012_11_en.pdf. Accessed 31 Jan 2012

European Commission (2012d) Proposal for a Directive of the European Parliament and of the Council on the protection of individuals with regard to the processing of personal data by competent authorities for the purposes of prevention, investigation, detection or prosecution of criminal offences or the execution of criminal penalties, and the free movement of such data. COM(2012) 10 final. http://ec.europa.eu/justice/data-protection/document/review2012/com_2012_10_en.pdf. Accessed 31 Jan 2012

European Parliament (1995) Directive 95/46/EC of the European Parliament and of the Council of 24 October 1995 on the Protection of Individuals with Regard to the Processing of Personal Data and on Free Movement of such Data. http://eur-lex.europa.eu/LexUriServ/LexUriServ.do?uri=OJ:L:1995:281:0031:0050:EN:PDF. Accessed 31 Jan 2012

European Parliament (2000) Charter of Fundamental Rights of the European Union. 2000/C 364/01. 18 Dec 2000. http://www.europarl.europa.eu/charter/default_en.htm. Accessed 31 Jan 2012

European Parliament (2002) Directive 2002/58/EC of the European Parliament and of the Council of 12 July 2002 Concerning the Processing of Personal Data and the Protection of Privacy in the Electronic Communications Sector (Directive on Privacy and Electronic Communications). http://eur-lex.europa.eu/LexUriServ/LexUriServ.do?uri=OJ:L:2002:201:0037:0047:EN:PDF. Accessed 31 Jan 2012

European Parliament (2006) Directive 2006/24/EC of the European Parliament and of the Council of 15 March 2006 on the Retention of Data Generated or Processed in Connection with the Provision of Publicly Available Electronic Communications Services or of Public

Communications Networks and Amending Directive 2002/58/. http://eur-lex.europa.eu/LexUriServ/LexUriServ.do?uri=OJ:L:2006:105:0054:0063:EN:PDF. Accessed 31 Jan 2013

European Parliament (2010) Information and Communication Technologies and Human Rights. http://www.europarl.europa.eu/committees/en/studiesdownload.html?languageDocument=EN&file=31731. Accessed 31 Jan 2012

European Union (2010) Consolidated Version of the Treaty on the Functioning of the European Union.http://eur-lex.europa.eu/LexUriServ/LexUriServ.do?uri=OJ:C:2010:083:0047:0200:en:PDF. Accessed 31 Jan 2012

German Federal Constitutional Court (2010) 1 BvR 256/08. 2 March 2010. http://www.bverfg.de/entscheidungen/rs20100302_1bvr025608.html. Accessed 31 Jan 2012

Gollwitzer W (2005) Menschenrechte im Strafverfahren: MRK und IPBPR. Commentary. Walter de Gruyter, Berlin

Grewlich KW (1999) Governance in "cyberspace": access and public interest in global communications. Kluwer Law International, The Hague

Hosein G (2006) Privacy as freedom. In: Jørgensen RF (ed) Human rights in the global information society. MIT Press, Cambridge

Jackson M (2011) Right to privacy, unlawful search and surveillance. In: Chan J, Lim CL (eds) Law of the Hong Kong constitution. Sweet and Maxwell, Hong Kong

Kang J (1998) Information privacy in cyberspace transactions. Stanford Law Rev 50(4):1193–1294

Martin K (2006) Privacy and anonymity, security focus. 14 Feb 2006. http://www.securityfocus.com/columnists/386. Accessed 31 Jan 2012

Marzouki M (2006) The "guarantee rights" for realizing the rule of law. In: Jørgensen RF (ed) Human rights in the global information society. MIT Press, Cambridge

Mayer-Schönberger V (2009) Delete: the virtue of forgetting in the digital age. Princeton University Press, Princeton

OECD (1980) Guidelines on the Protection of Privacy and Transborder Flows of Personal Data. 23 Sept 1980. http://www.oecd.org/document/18/0,3746,en_2649_34255_1815186_1_1_1_1,00&&en-USS_01DBC.html. Accessed 31 Jan 2012

OECD (2002) Guidelines for the Security of Information Systems and Networks: Towards a Culture of Security. 25 July 2002. http://www.oecd.org/dataoecd/16/22/15582260.pdf. Accessed 31 Jan 2012

OpenNet Initiative (2009) Internet Filtering in China. 15 June 2009. http://opennet.net/sites/opennet.net/files/ONI_China_2009.pdf. Accessed 31 Jan 2012

Orwell G (1949) 1984, London

Pätzold J (2012) Art. 8 EMRK. In: Karpenstein U., Mayer FC (eds) EMRK—Konvention zum Schutz der Menschenrechte und Grundfreiheiten. Commentary. C.H. Beck, Munich

Posner RA (1998) The right of privacy. Georgia Law Review 12(3):393–422

Reidenberg JR (2000) Resolving conflicting international data privacy rules in cyberspace. Stanford Law Rev 52(5):1315–1376

Solove DJ (2007) The future of reputation: gossip, rumor, and privacy on the internet. Yale University Press, New Haven

Trenkelbach H (2005) Internetfreiheit: Die Europäische Menschenrechtskonvention als "Living Instrument" vor neuen Herausforderungen?. Logos Verlag, Berlin

United Nations (1948) Universal Declaration of Human Rights, 10 December 1948. http://www.ohchr.org/en/udhr/pages/introduction.aspx. Accessed 31 Jan 2012

United Nations (1966) International Covenant on Civil and Political Rights. 16 Dec 1966. http://www2.ohchr.org/english/law/ccpr.htm. Accessed 31 Jan 2012

United Nations (1990) Guidelines for the Regulation of Computerized Personal Data Files. 14 December 1990. http://www.unhcr.org/refworld/publisher,UNGA,THEMGUIDE,,3ddcafaac,0.html. Accessed 31 Jan 2012

Volokh E (2000) Freedom of speech, cyberspace, harassment law, and the Clinton administration. Law Contemp Prob 63:299–335

Wacks R (2000) Law, moralty, and the private domain, Hong Kong

Warren S, Brandeis L (1890) The right to privacy. Harvard Law Rev 4(5):193–220
Weber RH (2002) Regulatory models for the online world. Schulthess, Zurich
Weber RH (2009) Internet governance: regulatory challenges. Schulthess, Zurich
Weber RH (2011a) The Right to Be Forgotten: More Than a Pandora's Box?. J Intellectual Property Inf Technol E-Commerce Law 2: 120–130
Weber RH (2012b) How Does Privacy Change in the Age of the Internet, In: Fuchs C, Boersma K, Albrechtslund A, Sandoval M (eds) Internet and Surveillance: The Challenges of Web 2.0 and Social Media. Routledge, New York
Weber RH, Sommerhalder M (2007) Das Recht der personenbezogenen Information. Schulthess/Nomos, Zurich
Wildhaber L, Breitenmoser S (1992) Art. 8 EMRK. In: Golsong H, Karl W (eds) Internationaler Kommentar zur Europäischen Menschenrechtskommission. Commentary. Carl Heymanns Verlag, Cologne

Chapter 4
Limitations of Anonymization

4.1 Factual Reasons for State Interventions

As previously mentioned, the Internet users' intentions to stay anonymous in the Internet are manifold and range from legal to a wide range of illegal reasons. Proponents of a right to stay anonymous on the Internet mainly rest their position on the protection of the individual's data and on privacy[1]; the opposing side calls for a transparent Internet enabling no anonymous acting on the Internet. For consolidating their positions the advocates of transparency refer to the ongoing violations of rights committed by Internet users curtaining their identity and therewith seeking for abdicating responsibility.

Recently, especially subsequently to the tragic events in Norway in summer 2011, voices were again being raised to completely stop anonymous acting on the Internet. On 22 July 2011 a Norwegian right-wing extremist accomplished two sequential terrorist attacks previously announced online with 77 people killed and many people injured; over a period of years prior to his attacks the Norwegian extremist had participated in Internet for a debating against immigration and the Islam and published a hate-filled manifesto by appearing on the scene anonymously, just using a pseudonym.[2]

Additionally, iterative hacker attacks of Internet users contribute to the revivification of the debate concerning the justification of a right to stay anonymous on the Internet. Within the last months repeatedly hacker attacks by individuals or groups hiding their IP addresses by using anonymizing services like proxy servers[3] acting among others under the pseudonym "Anonymous"[4] were reported pursuing

[1] See Chap. 3.
[2] Pseudonymity is characterized by the use of a false name and for the most part eventuates in anonymity; see Sect. 1.1.
[3] See Sect. 2.2.2.1(1).
[4] See Chap. 2, footnote 6.

R. H. Weber and U. I. Heinrich, *Anonymization*, SpringerBriefs in Cybersecurity,
DOI: 10.1007/978-1-4471-4066-5_4,

the objection of illegally penetrating large companies' data bases and spy out customer data or solely to harm companies by immobilizing their web pages.[5]

Hence, national policy and State security organisations have to also focus their attention to the actions taken within the virtual world, at least since the number of terrorist incidents has increased starting with the attacks of 11 September 2001 against the United States of America. During these devastating attacks terrorists hijacked four US passenger jets and misused them for conducting suicide outrages; thereby more than 3,000 people lost their life. The terrorists directed two passenger jets into the towers of the World Trade Centre in New York and the third one into the Pentagon in Arlington, Virginia; the fourth passenger jet was programmed to hit a government building in Washington D.C. but crashed earlier because of fights between hijacksers and passengers. In the forefront of the attacks the terrorists among others connected and communicated by (mis)using the anonymity of the Internet.

As a result of the attacks, governments all over the world enacted regulations to combat terrorism, partially including the authority to monitor telephone communications, email, and Internet use of terror suspects. Governments vindicate these measures with the fulfillment of their superordinate task of protecting their citizens and therewith acting in the public interest. Hence, this duty to protect its citizens and defeating offences is confronted with the individual's interest on privacy, as in the case of an acting anonymously on the Internet.

Since not all possible limitations of anonymity can be addressed, the following subchapters particularly shed light on State supervision in general, the combat of cybercrime, the supervision of Internet traffic by Trojan horse software and the enforcement of Internet copyright infringements as special case of illegal Internet activity.

4.2 State Supervision in the Public Interest in General

Generally looking, States do have an interest that the Internet is not used for illegal purposes. The respective risk is imminent since the Internet allows an individual quite easily to remain anonymous; as outlined, anonymity cannot anymore be protected if higher ranking objectives of a State require disclosure of information and transparency.

4.2.1 Legitimate State Interests

Several interests that can be invoked by States for interventions into the Internet traffic are legitimate. Indeed, the Internet is not a sphere being outside of the scope

[5] See exemplary attacks of "Anonymous" vs. Stratfor, Sect. 2.1.3.

of the legal framework at all. The proclamation of John Perry Barlow in his manifesto "A Declaration of the Independence of Cyberspace" of 1996 containing the sentence "You [governments] have no moral right to rule us, nor do you possess any methods of enforcement we have true reason to fear" (Barlow 1996) has obviously turned out to be wrong. Early legal scholars also assessed the legal situation in an improper way: "There is no regulatory body, and computers are capable of anything.[…] Since there is no regulatory body policing the Internet, the extent to which an individual is capable of speaking without restriction is an enigma" (Ryga 1995, pp. 221, 223).

The most obvious example for a legitimate state intervention is the interest of combating cybercrime.[6] Other reasons could be the realization of public order and public morals or the enforcement of property rights.[7]

Public order and public morals obviously depend on the given circumstances and the national appreciation of State interests. Therefore, a globally accepted definition of these terms is not available. Nevertheless, the WTO-law knows these terms, namely in Art. XX of the GATT (only public morals) and Art. XIV of the GATS (public order and public morals). In the field of the delivery of cross-border services, the dispute settlement bodies of the WTO have assessed these terms in two cases, namely the "US- Gambling case" and the "China—Publications and Audiovisual Products case":

- Public order "refers to the preservation of the fundamental interests of a society, as reflected in public policy and law. These fundamental interests can relate, inter alia, to standards of law, security and morality".[8] The focus is on societal interests, similar to those in international private law like fundamental values and concerns of the country's society (Cottier Delimatsis and Diebold 2008, p. 299, margin number 22).
- Public morals refer to "standards of right and wrong conduct maintained by or on behalf of a community or nation".[9] Public morals are influenced by each country's prevailing social, cultural, ethical and religious values.[10] Legal doctrine interprets "public morals" as encompassing measures relating to alcohol, sex, gambling, slavery, torture of animals and drugs (Cottier Delimatsis and Diebold 2008, p. 298, margin number 21).

---

6 See Sect. 4.3.

7 See Sect. 4.5.

8 United States—Measures affecting the cross-border supply of gambling and betting services (US—Gambling), WT/DS285/R, Panel Report, para 6.467.

9 Id. para 6.465.

10 China—Measures affecting trading rights and distribution services for certain publications and audiovisual entertainment products, WT/DS363/R, Panel Report, para 7.763.

Notwithstanding the fact that the two terms stand for two distinct concepts, some overlap exists; both terms seek to protect similar values.[11] Partly it is argued that public order is broader than public morals since it includes further interests such as safety and access to essential facilities (Munin 2010, p. 357). In the context of the anonymity assessment, however, the details of the relationship between public order and public morals (see for further details Cottier Delimatsis and Diebold 2008, p. 299) does not need to be elaborated further; moreover, the interpretation in the given situation of a State intervention as well as the fulfillment of general legal principles such as the necessity, proportionality and suitability of the measure are decisive.

Furthermore, international legal instruments regularly contain clauses allowing States to limit the exercise of fundamental rights; examples are

- Article 19 para 3 ICCPR (United Nations 1966) stating that "the exercise of the rights provided for in paragraph 2 of this article carries with it special duties and responsibilities. It may therefore be subject to certain restrictions, but these shall only be such as are provided by law and are necessary: (a) For respect of the rights or reputations of others; (b) For the protection of national security or of public order (ordre public), or of public health or morals."
- Article 8 para 2 ECHR (Council of Europe 1950)[12] stating that "there shall be no interference by a public authority with the exercise of this right except such as is in accordance with the law and is necessary in a democratic society in the interests of national security, public safety or the economic well-being of the country, for the prevention of disorder or crime, for the protection of health or morals, or for the protection of the rights and freedoms of others".

Summarizing, legitimate State interests can exist, justifying governmental intervention into the sphere of anonymization of individuals. As international legal instruments, however, show in different ways and in not identical words, the public order argument can only be legitimately invoked if a fundamental interest of a State calls for a specific measure. The respective rules, allowing interventions, must be interpreted in a narrow way in order to ensure that the individual protection regime will not be undermined over time.

4.2.2 Legal Bases for State Interventions

4.2.2.1 Determination of Scope of Human Rights

State interventions into the Internet traffic jeopardize the exercise of human rights. The most important rights are the freedom of expression and the right to privacy.

---

[11] US—Gambling, supra note 9, para 6.468.

[12] See Sect. 3.1.3.1.

The mentioned two human rights themselves can come into a direct conflict since an unlimited freedom of expression most likely interferes with privacy interests and an unlimited right to privacy makes the free exchange of communication in the Internet hardly possible.[13]

The new Internet age also calls for the development of new fundamental rights which are suitable to more precisely deal with the particularities of the most recent communication channels. In fact, this way has been chosen by the German Federal Constitutional Court having designed and accepted a so-called "computer confidentiality and integrity right" (German Federal Constitutional Court 2008) within its ruling of February 27, 2008.

The constitutional complaints in question[14] were both based on the doubted constitutionality of regulations of a regional Protection of the Constitution Act (in particular, Article 5 para 2 No. 11 Protection of the Constitution Act of North Rhine-Westphalia) authorizing public authorities (for the protection of the constitution) to secretly monitoring the Internet and, beyond that, secretly accessing information technology systems and thus realizing an online surveillance[15] of suspects. Within its ruling the German Federal Constitutional Court declared the confidentiality and integrity of personal data in information technology systems (private computers, smart phones, etc.) of being a fundamental right comparable to the inviolability of the home (German Federal Constitutional Court 2008: guiding principle No. 1; Rosenbach Stark and Winter 2011) and ruled the secret infiltration of these systems of being an infringement of the general personality right (German Federal Constitutional Court 2008: Sect. 166).

For being constitutionally legitimate, the secret infiltration presupposes circumstantial evidence of the existence of a concrete danger to a legally protected interest of outstanding importance, namely a person's life, limb and freedom, or goods of the community whose menace concern theSstate's fundamentals/existence or the existence of mankind (German Federal Constitutional Court 2008: guiding principle No. 2). However, according to the judgement the secret reconnaissance requires a court order to protect the suspect's "core area of private way of life"; the court order must be based on a law containing precautionary measures to protect the aforementioned core area (German Federal Constitutional Court 2008: guiding principle No. 3).

As outlined, the mentioned international legal instruments know quite similar conditions that must be met in order to make a state intervention legitimate.

---

[13] See Chap. 3.

[14] The group of appellants consists of a journalist, an active politician and two associates of a law firm (German Federal Constitutional Court 2008: Sects. 116–118) who blamed a personality right violation, precisely a violation of the fundamental right in confidentiality and integrity of information technology systems, also referred to as "right to online privacy" or "computer confidentiality and integrity right" (Weber 2011a, p. 128); for an evaluation of this decision see Weber 2008, pp. 94–97.

[15] See Chap. 3, footnote 8.

4.2.2.2 Conditions for State Interventions

A first condition for a State intervention is regularly the formal requirement of having a law in place. Police authorities, for instance in a envisaged criminal prosecution, are not entitled to break into a privacy or anonymity right if the respective action cannot be based on a law formally enacted. Usually, the law has been passed by the parliament, a governmental ordinance is not sufficient. Furthermore, the law must describe with sufficient clarity under which circumstances a state intervention is legitimate.[16] Obviously, the assessment of the quality of law depends on the national legislator; in addition, the lack of a law might be remedied by the enactment of a new legal provision.

A second condition of substantive nature addresses the necessity of the State intervention: The chosen governmental activity has to be proportionate to the envisaged objective of the intervention. Consequently, the measure should not exceed the required limitation of an individual's human right; a balance of interests test (Jackson 2011: 21.029) has to be applied evaluating the corresponding motivations and expectations of the concerned persons/entities.[17]

A third condition concerns the suitability of a governmental measure, thereby including a procedural element: The intervention of the State must be appropriate in view of the envisaged objective being suitable to achieve it in the best possible manner.[18] The European Court of Human Rights refers to "pressing social needs"[19] in the interpretation of the proportionality and the suitability principle.

In addition, the general interpretation principle applies that limitations and restrictions related to the exercise of human rights are to be interpreted in a narrow way, i.e. the legitimacy of state interventions based on the necessity test (proportionality and suitability criteria) must be submitted to a strong assessment[20] of the fulfillment of its conditions.[21]

Recently, a further aspect related to the scope of human rights has been more intensively debated, namely the question whether and, if yes, to what extent human rights have a (minimal) core protection which cannot be touched and limited at all.

---

16 ECHR: Autronic AG vs. Switzerland, judgment of 22 May 1990, No. 17/1989/175/231, § 57; Rekvényi vs. Hungary, judgment of 20 May 1999, No. 25390/94, § 34.

17 ECHR, The Sunday Times I vs. The United Kingdom (Series A No. 30), judgment of 26 April 1979, §§ 54 ss.

18 ECHR: Handyside vs. The United Kingdom, judgment of 7 June 1976, No. 5493/72, § 46; The Sunday Times I vs. United Kingdom (Series A No 30), judgment of 26 April 1979, § 59; The Observer and Guardian vs. The United Kingdom, judgment of 26 November 1991, No. 13585/88, § 59; Krone Verlag GmbH & Co. KG vs. Asustria, judgment of 26 February 2002, No. 34315/96, § 34.

19 ECHR, Dichand and Others vs. Austria, judgment of 26 February 2002, No. 29271/95, § 1.

20 ECHR: The Observer and Guardian vs. The United Kingdom, judgment of 26 November 1991, No. 13585/88, § 59; Thoma vs. Luxembourg, judgment of 29 March 2001, No. 38432/97, § 43; Perna vs. Italy, judgment of 25 July 2001, No. 48898/99, § 38.

21 Non-consensual "searches" of a person are illegal unless authorized by law, i.e. by legislation or as a matter of common law, comp. Jackson 2011: 21.082.

In fact, some Constitutions (for example Germany, Art. 19 para 2 of the Basic Law, or Switzerland, Art. 36 para 4 of the Constitution) know the principle of a core protection of some human rights (see Schefer 2001). State (and private) interventions into this core protection are illegal and can be challenged. For obvious reasons, the scope of the core protection depends on the given societal perceptions of the concerned State. In practical terms, a law forbidding any communication in an anonymous way might not be compliant with the human right to privacy.

Similar concepts can also be derived from international legal instruments: According to the Human Rights Committee, interpreting the International Covenant on Civil and Political Rights of 1966, reasons of public interest "may never be invoked as a justification for the muzzling of any advocacy of multi-party democracy, democratic tenets and human rights".[22] The European Court of Human Rights also stated that a minimal scope of human rights would be inherent to a democracy and interference into such scope would not be justified by pressing social needs (Wildhaber and Breitenmoser 1992: margin number 729). Looking at State interventions into the free flow of traffic in the Internet it seems to be worth to look more closely into the possibility of applying the described core protection concept in the future.

4.2.2.3 Positive Obligations of States

During the last few years the question has been more intensively debated whether States would have so-called positive obligations to actually guarantee the possibility for individuals to fully realize the human rights. The purpose of such an understanding consists in the objective to avoid interference into human rights by private actors. As far as the right to privacy and to confidentiality is concerned, the European Court of Human Rights (ECHR) has approved and requested the existence of positive obligations in several court decisions.[23]

In particular, the ECHR stated under the heading of "general principles" in a decision rendered in 2003[24]: "Effective exercise of this freedom does not depend merely on the State's duty not to interfere, but may require positive measures of protection, even in the sphere of relations between individuals". Furthermore, the

[22] Human Rights Committee, International Covenant on Civil and Political Rights, 102nd Session, 12 September 2011, CCPR-C-GC/34, No. 23.

[23] ECHR: Kegan vs. Irland, judgment of 26 May 1994, No. 16969/90, § 49; McGinley and Egan vs. The United Kingdom, judgment of 9 June 1998, No. 10/1997/794/995–996, § 98; Guerra and Others vs. Italy, judgment of 19 February 1998, No. 14967/89, § 58; Christine Goodwin vs. The United Kingdom, judgment of 11 July 2002, No. 28957/95, §§ 71/2; compare also Weber and Sommerhalder 2007, p. 97.

[24] ECHR, Appleby and Others vs. The United Kingdom, judgment of 6 May 2003, No. 44306/98, § 39/40.

ECHR held[25]: "In determining whether or not a positive obligation exists, regard must be had to the fair balance that has to be struck between the general interest of the community and the interests of the individual".

An interest of having the State intervening if an individual limits the exercise of a human right of another individual is particularly given of the restrictive activity cannot be based on legitimate reasons: If an Internet Service Provider permanently violates privacy rights of customers, an adequate interest balancing test would have to cause the State to intervene and prohibit the activity of the ISP not complying with privacy principles.

4.3 Combating Cybercrime

4.3.1 Subject Matter of Protection

As mentioned the World Wide Web offers manifold information and communication possibilities which are not necessarily compliant with the addressed (controversial) right to act anonymously therein. Notwithstanding the respective tensions, criminal activities committed through electronic channels due to the fact that the Information and Communication Technologies' (ICT) are developing are becoming "easier" and, therefore, the number of cybercrime cases and other criminal offences being executed based on telecommunication or public communication networks are increasing which is socially undesirable (Moore 2011, p. 4). Examples are data theft, identity theft, distribution of child pornography or copyright infringements.[26] For hampering the criminal prosecution a standard practice is to mask the used IP address (Graham, Howard and Olson 2011, p. 75). As a consequence, cyberspace, also referred to as the fifth common space,[27] "is in great need for coordination, cooperation and legal measures among all nations" (Schjølberg 2011, p. 2).

However, while some actions may be illegal in one part of the world, they may be legal in another area of the world since each State's national legislation differs from the one of other States. In this respect, the online world is similar to the offline world. Furthermore, with regard to the fact that access to the Internet can be achieved from almost every place on earth providing the necessary facilities, offenders very often operate from another part of the world (Moore 2011, p. 260). This aspect brings along further difficulties regarding the criminal prosecution: which States' relevant legislation will be applied in practice?

---

[25] ECHR, Appleby and Others vs. The United Kingdom, judgment of 6 May 2003, No. 44306/98, § 40.

[26] For more detailed information regarding the enforcement of copyright see Sect. 4.5.

[27] The four other spaces are land, sea, air and outer space.

Being a global problem, cybercrime must be understood from a global perspective. Effective cybercrime laws that are enforceable at national and international levels within a global and harmonized legal framework need to be developed, taking into account the Internet users' privacy. Insofar, public awareness of cybercrime and cybersecurity challenges will help to promote a cybersecurity culture.

Up to now, different efforts have been undertaken like the International Telecommunication Union's (ITU) Global Cybercrime Agenda, the subsequently founded ITU High-Level Expert Group, the Council of Europe's Convention on Cybercrime and several Framework Decisions and Directives of the European Union as set out hereinafter.

4.3.2 Global Cybersecurity Agenda

4.3.2.1 International Telecommunication Union

With governments realizing the growing importance of the new information and communication services, the International Telecommunication Union (ITU) passed a resolution in 1998 proposing the idea of a World Summit on the Information Society (WSIS) under the auspices of the United Nations. In 2001, the ITU Council endorsed the approach of holding the Summit in two phases, the first one in Geneva in 2003, the second one in Tunis two years later.

Being the United Nations specialized agency for information and communication technologies,[28] the ITU's activities focus on three main areas of activity, namely radio communication, standardization and development. In particular, the ITU coordinates the shared global use of the radio spectrum, promotes international cooperation in assigning satellite orbits, works to improve telecommunication infrastructure in the developing world and establishes worldwide standards.

Both World Summits on the Information Society highlighted security as a main pillar for building a stable global information society (Weber 2009, pp. 31–36). Hence, the ITU together with partners from governments, industry, international organisations and civil society launched the Global Cybersecurity Agenda (GCA) on 17 May 2007 (ITU 2007, p. 5), seeking to encourage collaboration amongst all relevant partners (HLEG 2008, p. 1). In so doing, serious crimes in cyberspace should be established under international law, regardless of whether they are chargeable under the respective national law (Schjølberg 2011, p. 2).

Following the idea of coordinating the international response to the growing challenges to cybersecurity and thereby aiming at proposing solutions to enhance confidence and security in the use of ICT (ITU 2007, p. 5), the GCA was built on

[28] See homepage of the ITU, overview.

five strategic pillars, namely legal aspects, technical measures, organisational structures, capacity building and international cooperation (ITU 2007, p. 13).

The GCA's central element is the establishment of a High-Level Experts Group (HLEG) aiming at refining the initial items listed on the Cybercrime Agenda (ITU 2007, p. 16); in particular the following objectives should be achieved: (1) the development of a model cybercrime legislation and a strategy to establish globally accepted minimum security criteria and accreditation schemes for software applications and systems taking into account existing public and private initiatives, (2) the creation and endorsement of a generic policy model and national strategies to develop appropriate national and regional structures to deal with cybercrime, (3) the establishment of a framework for watch, warning and incidents response, (4) the creation and endorsement of a universal generic identity framework to ensure the recognition of digital credentials for citizens across geographical boundaries, (5) the development of a global strategy to facilitate human and institutional capacity building and (6) the establishment of a global multi-stakeholder strategy to support and promote international cooperation for reaching all these goals mentioned above.

4.3.2.2 High-Level Experts Group

In order to fulfil the GCA's objectives the said High-Level Experts Group (HLEG) was established in 2007. Consisting of more than 100 experts from the fields of policy-making, academia, government and even the private sector (HLEG 2008, p. 2) the HLEG is subdivided into five working groups among others dealing with legislation, technological aspects, organisational aspects and the international cooperation among the Members.

To serve the Expert Group's main purpose of using "recognized sources of expertise in order to develop and propose practical solutions to facilitate the achievement of well-defined ITU strategic goals in cyberspace" (ITU 2007, p. 18), already in September 2008 the HLEG delivered a Chairman's Report (HLEG 2008, p. 191), comprising specific recommendations on cybercrime legislations by putting forward strategies regarding the aforementioned five work areas (ITU 2007, p. 16; HLEG 2008, p. 4). Additionally, the HLEG delivered a Global Strategic Report in November 2008,[29] including strategies in the five[30] work areas and summarizing the HLEG's work in seeking to promote cybersecurity around the world.

---

[29] HLEG Global Strategic Report 2008, http://www.itu.int/osg/csd/cybersecurity/gca/docs/global_strategic_report.pdf.

[30] The five work areas are legal measures, technical and procedural measures, organisational structures, capacity building and international cooperation, see supra note 30.

4.3.2.3 Implementation of the Global Cybersecurity Agenda

Since the GCA's launch in 2007, the composition has attracted the support and recognition of States and cybersecurity experts around the world and has promoted a number of initiatives, such as the ITU Child Online Protection Initiative that has been established in 2008 as an international collaborative network to promote the online protection of children worldwide by providing guidance on safe online behaviour.[31]

During the 2011 World Summit for Information Society Forum in Geneva, the ITU signed an agreement with the International Multilateral Partnership Against Cyber Threats (IMPACT), a not-for-profit comprehensive global public–private partnership alliance against cyber threats, making IMPACT the cybersecurity executing arm of the ITU as of September 9, 2011.[32] Being tasked with the responsibility of providing cybersecurity assistance and support to ITU's 193 Member States and also to other organisations within the UN system the ITU's GCA in collaboration with IMPACT is deploying security solutions to countries around the world.

4.3.3 Cybercrime Convention of Council of Europe

Since a harmonizing solution to combat cybercrime is needed, on the regional level already in 2001 the Council of Europe Convention on Cybercrime (Council of Europe 2004), the first international treaty seeking to address computer crime and Internet crimes by harmonizing national laws, appeared on the scene.

Having been developed between 1997 and 2000 by the Committee of Experts on Crime in Cyberspace (Gercke 2011, p. 142) the Convention on Cybercrime, also known as Budapest Convention on Cybercrime, was adopted by the Committee of Ministers of the Council of Europe on 8 November 2001 and entered into force on 1 July 2004. Later on, the Convention on Cybercrime was completed

---

[31] The ITU launched the Child Online Protection Initiative together with several UN agencies. The initiative's key objectives are among others the identification of risks to children in cyberspace, the creation of awareness and the development of practical tools for minimizing risks; see http://www.itu.int/osg/csd/cybersecurity/gca/cop/.

[32] The ITU considered the collaboration as "the world's first comprehensive alliance against cyberthreats"; see speech by ITU Secretary-General Dr Hamadoun I. Touréhttp, opening ceremony of the WSIS Forum, 16 May 2011, http://www.itu.int/en/osg/speeches/Pages/2011-05-16.aspx.

by the Additional Protocol to the Convention on cybercrime (Additional Protocol) (Council of Europe 2006),[33] entering into force on 1 March 2006.[34]

Seeking to "pursue, as a matter of priority, a common criminal policy aimed at the protection of society against cybercrime, inter alia, by adopting appropriate legislation and fostering international co-operation" (Council of Europe 2004: preamble), the Convention on Cybercrime aims at harmonizing the Member Countries' criminal regulations among others focussing on high-technology crimes such as illegal hacking into computer systems (Article 5), data piracy (Article 3), copyright infringements (Article 10), forgery and fraud (Article 7, 8), and the manufacture and distribution of child pornography (Article 9).

The Convention on Cybercrime serves as a guideline or as a reference for developing internal legislation by implementing its standards and principles in accordance with the local legal system and practice.[35] For standardizing the variety of national criminal regulations, to date, 47 States signed the Convention, even though just 32 States ratified the Convention. This numerical discrepancy among others refers to the fact that some of the Cybercrime Convention's criminalized actions are in conflict with the legal assessment of some Member States (Moore 2011, p. 261). By way of example, Article 5 of the Additional Protocol to the Convention on Cybercrime (Council of Europe 2006) is criminalizing hate speech; this legal provision might contradict the United States' First Amendment's guarantee of free speech[36]; similar legal problems occur related to the issue of child pornography (Moore 2011, p. 261).

Being based on criminal cyber-conducts in the late 1990s the Convention on Cybercrime does not cover new methods of conduct in cyberspace with criminal intent, such as phishing, botnets, spam, identity theft, crime in virtual worlds, terrorist use of the Internet, and massive and coordinated cyber-attacks against information infrastructures. In addition, the terminology included in the Convention turns out to be a 1990s terminology which is not necessarily suitable for the second decade of the 21st century. Hence, with regard to the use of anonymizing services[37] on the Internet the Convention on Cybercrime contains no specific regulations; the Convention "solely" introduces a regulatory framework for its Member Countries to handle criminal actions related to the World Wide Web.

---

[33] The Additional Protocol to the Convention on Cybercrime was adopted by the Council of Europe Committee of Ministers on 7 November 2002, open also to non-CoE-countries.

[34] States having ratified the Additional Protocol are requested to criminalize the dissemination of racist and xenophobic material and xenophobic-motivated threats and results through computer systems.

[35] Schjølberg and Ghernaouti-Hélie 2009 with a detailed proposal for a preliminary Model Law on Cybercrime Legislation based on the recommendations that were adopted in a broad agreement by the global High-Level Experts Group on Cybersecurity (for HLEG see 4.3.2.2), and recommendations on additional provisions due to the technological development since 2001.

[36] For more details regarding the U.S. Supreme Court's standpoint regarding the relationship between the First Amendment and defamation see Solove 2007, p. 125.

[37] See Sect. 2.2.

However, the Convention on Cybercrime also encompasses regulations allowing for a greater cooperation between law enforcement agencies and Internet Service Providers (ISPs) by determining the conditions in which ISPs are obliged to provide information (Moore 2011, p. 261) about their user to government agents (Article 18 para 1 lit. b Convention on Cybercrime). Due to the fact that anonymous acting on the Internet and the disclosure of information concerning a specific Internet user are inconsistent with one another, making reference to the Convention on Cybercrime is not that suitable to justify a right to act anonymously on the Internet.

4.3.4 EU Agenda

For the Council of Europe's (CoE's) non-Member Countries the Convention on Cybercrime serves as a central source to bring these countries' legislation towards European standards (Gercke 2011, p. 143). With regard to the CoE's Convention of Cybercrime's practical relevance for Member States of the EU, within the last ten years the EU has developed a number of legal frameworks for advancing the fight against cybercrime, among others the (1) Framework Decision on Combating Fraud (Council of the European Union 2001), (2) the Framework Decision on Attacks against Information Systems (Council of the European Union 2005), (3) the European Data Retention Directive (European Parliament 1995) and the (4) Amendment of the Framework Decision on Combating Terrorism (Council of the European Union 2008). Unlike the Council of Europe combining 47 Member States, all 27 Member States of the EU have to implement the aforementioned EU instruments within a given time frame (Gercke 2011, p. 143).

1. The Framework Decision on Combating Fraud of 2001 aims at assisting the European Union's fight against fraud and counterfeiting involving non-cash means of payment (Council of the European Union 2001: considerations 1, 5).[38] Therefore, the Framework Decision on Combating Fraud obligates all Member States to implement necessary measures to ensure the liability of legal persons intentionally committing one of the criminal offences listed in Article 2, as for instance theft or counterfeiting of a payment instrument in order for it to be used fraudulently.
2. Later on in 2005 the Framework Decision on Attacks against Information Systems was adopted, pursuing the goal to advance the cooperation between judicial and other competent authorities in the area of attacks against information systems (Council of the European Union 2005: consideration 1), by obliging all Member States "to take the necessary measures to ensure that the

[38] Fraud and counterfeiting of non-cash means of payment often operate on an international scale.

intentional access without right to the whole ore any part of an information system is punishable as a criminal offence" (Article 2) within the given transition period.

3. Subsequently, the European Parliament and the Council of the European Union adopted the Data Retention Directive, as set out above, aiming at harmonising all Member States' regulations for establishing a framework to enable law enforcement authorities and intelligence agencies to access stored communications, traffic and location data, thereby improving criminal investigations.
4. Furthermore, the Amendment of the Framework Decision on Combating Terrorism needs to be mentioned, updating the Council Framework Decision of 13 June 2002 on Combating Terrorism. Including new offences, namely public provocation to commit a terrorist offence, recruitment and training for terrorism, also when committed through the World Wide Web, the Amendment and the underlying Framework Decision constitute a key tool in the fight against terrorism and aim at harmonizing respective national provisions.

Similarly to the Convention on Cybercrime, the EU Framework Decision on Combating Fraud, the Framework Decision on Attacks against Information Systems, the Data Retention Directive and the Amendment of the Framework Decision on Combating Terrorism do not contain specific conditions to substantiate a right to act anonymously on the Internet (by using anonymizers). In fact, a justification of such a right would adversely affect the Framework Decisions' and Directive's fundamental idea of improving prosecution in the case of criminal actions committed on the Internet.

4.4 Supervising Internet Traffic by Trojan Horse Software

4.4.1 Use of Trojan Horse Software by the German Government

In the context of conflicting interests between the Internet participants' privacy and the States' duty to protect governments partially draw on illegal measures, as shown by the German Chaos Computer Club (CCC)[39] in respect of the recently

[39] Claiming to be the "largest European hacker club" (CCC 2011a), the German hacker association CCC founded in Berlin, Germany, in 1981 and based in Germany and other German-speaking countries assesses itself as a mediator between the poles of technical and social development. According to its preamble, the CCC urges for the appreciation of the right to a worldwide, unhampered information exchange as being a human right since within today's information society living and working without Internet access is almost inconceivable (CCC 2011b). Furthermore, the CCC stands up for more transparency in governments, freedom of information and fights for everyman's right for free universal access to computers and technological infrastructure. The political activities of the Chaos Computer Club bear on the revelation of shortcomings and the disclosure of security loopholes, partially by intentionally breaking through existing safety appliances as undertaken in 1996 by demonstrating an attack against Microsoft's ActiveX technology.

revealed potentially unconstitutional use of Trojan horse software by German investigators. In addition to this occurrence also other governments made use of the Trojan horse software.

4.4.1.1 Trojan Horse Software

(1) Trojan Horse Mythology

According to the Greek mythology, within the Trojan War the Greeks finally entered the city of Troy and ended the conflict by outflanking the Trojans. The Greeks constructed a huge wooden horse, presented it to the Trojans and made the Trojans belief that they sailed away. Thereupon, the Trojans opened their gates and pulled the horse into their city unknowingly that they let the enemy in since the Greeks had hidden a select force of men inside the horse. In the course of the following night the Greeks came out of the horse, opened the gates for the rest of their secretly resailed army and overwhelmed the sleeping Trojans.

(2) Trojan Horse Software

Referring to the aforementioned incident of Greek warriors sneaking inside the city of Troy (Moore 2011, p. 38), "Trojan Horse Software" (also referred to as Trojans)[40] means a computer program not knowingly installed by the computer's user that appears at a first glance as a useful program but performs a different task unknown to the person concerned (Graham Howard and Olson 2011, p. 92).[41]

The Trojan himself is not a computer virus and is not necessarily harmful. However, this software is often combined with further malicious software or enables malicious software to get onto the computer unnoticed, as for example so-called keyloggers that records keyboard or mouse movements and thus collect unencrypted data and passwords. Therefore, Trojans belong to the so-called malware, the unsolicited and harmful programs.[42]

The Trojan Horse Software's installation happens by the safety authority through physical access to the communication device or by the users themselves, either undetected via an email attachment (Moore 2011, p. 38)[43] or as a result of fraudulent representations in terms of the respective purpose of use (Braun and Roggenkamp 2011, p. 681). In both cases applications are installed on the

---

40 Even though this description is misleading since the Greeks finessed the Trojans and not vice versa.

41 As for instance applications that pretend to be antivirus programs.

42 See R. Moir, Defining Malware: FAQ, 1 October 2003, http://technet.microsoft.com/en-us/library/dd632948.aspx.

43 Trojan horses are often sent to a computers via email to legitimate users of the system.

communication devices of the persons concerned without their knowledge and their consent. The Trojans among others may be programmed to activate when an executive instruction is given to start a particular computer program or when the recipient of the contaminated email unwittingly activates the file (Moore 2011, p. 38).

The installation and activation of the malware enables the hacker to have access to the computer remotely and perform various operations like eavesdropping the complete Internet communication, down- or uploading of files, installation of software/further malware on the "captured" computer, or committing data theft by emailing password lists to the owner of the Trojan program (Moore 2011, p. 38). Insofar, Trojans have all the attributes to accomplish both a lawful interception[44] and the more extensive online surveillance.[45]

4.4.1.2 The German "Bundestrojaner"

(1) Disclosure by the Chaos Computer Club

According to the Chaos Computer Club, the software, reportedly developed by a Hessian company,[46] was among others used by Bavarian law-enforcement[47] officials and was played into the hackers' hands without being asked (CCC 2011c, p. 1). Having examined the transmitted German governmental software in detail, the Chaos Computer Club on 8 October 2011 disclosed the use of a "lawful interception malware program by German police forces" (CCC 2011a), since then better known as the Bundestrojaner or Staatstrojaner, a Federal Trojan horse software.[48]

---

[44] The often used term lawful interception, also referred to as wiretapping, directly at the source ("source wiretapping") (CCC 2011a) of the communication, describes the monitoring of a suspect's Internet telephony by accessing to one of the end-devices involved using Trojan horse software. By definition, this procedure can only be used for wiretapping Internet telephony; the solely usage for conducting a lawful interception has to be enforced by appropriate technical and legal means (CCC 2011a). Moreover, for the protection of the overheard person's human rights, the conduct of a lawful interception requires a warrant; the Global Lawful Interception Industry Forum lists many of these different legislations, as does the Council of Europe secretariat. For example, in the United Kingdom the law is known as RIPA (Regulation of Investigatory Powers Act) and in the United States there is an array of federal and state criminal law, in particular the Communications Assistance for Law Enforcement Act (CALEA).

[45] See supra note 36.

[46] The investigated Trojan was developed by the company DigiTask; see exemplary Rosenbach, Stark and Winter 2011.

[47] The software in question was used by various state officials, see exemplary Rosenbach Stark and Winter 2011; German news agency 2011.

[48] The term "Bundestrojaner" is colloquially used to describe the government malware concept (CCC 2011a). The software is also referred to as R2D2, see exemplary: http://cetatti.com/blog/2011/10/german-officials-admit-to-using-r2d2-trojan-to-spy-on-citizens/.

Primarily, the computer surveillance program "Bundestrojaner" was developed to monitor suspects' Internet telephone calls via providers like Skype, a software application allowing its users to make partially free[49] telephone calls (voice and video) over the Internet. Since Internet telephony programs usually encrypt the data before they leave the sender's computer, the monitoring of the suspect's computer requires the controller's access to one of the end-devices involved (Braun and Roggenkamp 2011, p. 681).

Officially, the Trojan horse software was designed for the use on Windows operating systems for the recording of Voice over Internet Protocol (VoIP) telephone calls and for making screenshots of the reviewed computers, i.e. for accomplishing lawful interceptions of suspects.[50]

After having been passed the software in question, the CCC published the extracted binary files of the applied software used by the German investigators on their website (CCC 2011a), complemented by a report about the range of functions and an evaluation of the technical analysis (Braun and Roggenkamp 2011, p. 681). Subsequently, the CCC received a newer version (CCC 2011d) of the government spyware, publishing her findings on October 26, 2011 (CCC 2011e).

The first version of the Bundestrojaner passed to the Chaos Computer Club was assigned for wiretapping suspects' Internet telephone calls and for making screenshots of the reviewed computers (CCC 2011c, p. 2). As appears from the CCC's reports, the developed malware contains further functions which can easily be activated afterwards and enables the respective operator to install and run software on the tapped computer, monitor the online activity of the infected computer, scan and even manipulate the data stored on the computer and update its functionality via the Internet (CCC 2011c, p. 2).[51] Even though the later passed federal Trojan's basic version does no longer contain the possibility to copy the screenshot of the suspect's computer, the malware's range of application can be extended easily (CCC 2011f).

Hence, the said software has all the attributes to accomplish an online surveillance; beyond that even electronic eavesdropping operation (room surveillance) is possible by activating the computer's hardware (camera and/or microphone) from a distance (CCC 2011a). Since the Trojan's design and implementations involves the risk of "making all the functionality available to anyone on the Internet", the device uncloses a security loophole on the suspect's computer (CCC 2011a).

According to the CCC, this additional application's spectrum (over and above lawful interception) was "hidden" within the software on purpose as to enable the

---

[49] Telephone calls made by using the software application "Skype" to a recipient simultaneously using the application "Skype" are free of charge. Additionally, "Skype" enables its users to do instant messaging, to transfer files and to do videoconferencing over the Internet.

[50] See supra note 45.

[51] Beyond that the Bundestrojaner is said to be capable of monitoring traffic from 15 programs, see Constantin 2011.

enlargement of the suspects' spy out on demand beyond the allowed without additional judicial writ (CCC 2011c, p. 11, 15).

The server's IP address linking to a computer belonging to an US American computer center was firmly fixed "within" the Trojan software.[52] As a result, all tracked data were delivered to the United States first before they reached the respective German authorities (Tschentscher 2011, p. 21). Even though all data transmitted have been encoded, security gaps cannot be avoided since the same code was deployed within all examined versions of the software (Braun and Roggenkamp 2011, p. 682). Furthermore, a codification of inbound commands and a control of whether all these commands really originated from the US American server did not take place making the network's fraudulent manipulation technically possible.[53] Reportedly, installations of spyware utilized by German investigators were accomplished at the terminal device, some of them secretly during a customs control (Rosenbach et al. 2011; Braun and Roggenkamp 2011, p. 681).

In the course of the Trojan's disclosure by the CCC the issue was debated which technologies German law-enforcement officials are allowed to apply while investigating suspected criminals (Rosenbach et al. 2011) and if so whether the usage is undermining the ruling set in place by the February 27, 2008 German Federal Constitutional Court Ruling on the subject of online surveillance (German Federal Constitutional Court 2008), among others ruling the secret infiltration of information technology systems of being an infringement of the general personality right.[54]

(2) Legal Consequences of Malware Utilization

Due to the fact that there is no respective statutory rule existing in the German Code of Criminal Procedure,[55] the accomplishment of online surveillances for criminal prosecution is de lege lata illegitimate (Braun and Roggenkamp 2011, p. 682). According to the German Constitutional Court the accomplishment of source wiretapping also poses a threat to the basic law on IT, since the required infiltration of a computer effectively removes the crucial hurdle to spy out the information technology system at all (German Federal Constitutional Court 2008: Sect. 204).

Accordingly, the accomplishment of a lawful interception also requires a specific parent act (Braun and Roggenkamp 2011, p. 683 with further references). In this respect, the opinions are divided as to whether a source wiretapping can be based on the parent act of an "ordinary" telephone surveillance. While court

[52] The command and control server is located on an IP address belonging to the provider Web intellects in Columbus, Ohio; (CCC 2011c, p. 3).

[53] Hence, the networks remote control and tempering by third parties cannot be precluded; (CCC 2011c, p. 4).

[54] See Sect. 4.2.2.

[55] The German Code of Criminal Procedure (StPO).

practice and the legal doctrine partly base source wiretapping on Articles 100 a, b German Code of Criminal Procedure, the fact that telephone surveillances does not require access to the target subject's computer inter alia contradicts the equal treatment (Braun and Roggenkamp 2011, p. 683 with further references).

The Bundestrojaner's[56] legitimacy requires the existence of both software in conformity with the law and a provision authorizing the measure which is in accordance with the Constitutional Court Ruling (Braun and Roggenkamp 2011, p. 686).

Supposed, the legitimacy of using Trojans in general can be based on the German Code of Criminal Procedure, the application of the respective versions investigated by the CCC might have been unlawful (Braun and Roggenkamp 2011, p. 684). Basic principles of data protection law have been neglected since the tracked data passed unsecured networks (CCC 2011c, p. 6). Furthermore, with regard to the aforementioned missing parent act, the Trojan's implementation for accomplishing online surveillances was illegitimate.

Fuelled by the CCC's decryption of the Bundestrojaner the debate about Internet monitoring including the discussion about the right to remain and act anonymous on the Internet reaches a new intensity (Tschentscher 2011, p. 279). In consideration of the public debate about the existence and risk of terrorist structures within the right-wing scene[57] and the concomitant repeated calls for a party ban of the NPD[58] the Court Ruling on online surveillance could become subject to reconsideration in the future.

4.4.2 Use of Trojan Horse Software by Other Governments

4.4.2.1 Switzerland

Besides Germany also Switzerland[59] admitted the purchase and using of a particular type of computer spy software currently stirring debate in Germany (Weber et al. 2012, p. 6).[60]

Following the detection of the repeated use of Federal Trojans by German authorities and the subsequent concession of Swiss criminal prosecution authorities of having applied similar measures for conducting Internet surveillances, the Swiss Federal Council aims at precisely regulating the dealing with monitoring software. Since there is to date some disagreement about the existence of a legal

---

[56] For accomplishing lawful interceptions and online surveillances.

[57] In November 2011, German authorities discovered a neo-Nazi terror cell in Germany.

[58] The National Democratic Party of Germany is a far-right political party in Germany.

[59] Miscellaneous contributions in Swiss newspapers, see exemplary Schaffner 2011, p. 4 or Fontana 2011, p. 12.

[60] See Tschentscher 2011 and miscellaneous online contributions exemplary: http://www.eurasiareview.com/15102011-switzerland-law-enforcement-admits-use-of-spy-software/ and http://worldradio.ch/wrs/news/wrsnews/switzerland-admits-using-spy-software~print.shtml.

basis, the Swiss Federal Council plans to submit a draft proposal for the revision (Swiss Federal Data Protection Commissioner 2010/2011) of the Federal Law on the Surveillance of Postal and Telecommunications Traffic (Federal Assembly of the Swiss Confederation 2000), thereby creating more legal stability in dealing with Federal Trojans.

To date, Switzerland does not know a comparable right to the German right to confidentiality and integrity of information technology systems (Tschentscher 2011; Weber 2008). Instead, the surveillance of private computers with the aid of Trojans can affect a variety of fundamental rights, like for instance data protection, privacy, confidentiality of communication and personal liberty (Federal Constitution of the Swiss Confederation 1999; Tschentscher 2011). In contrast to the legal situation in Germany, the Swiss Federal Constitution in Article 13 codifies the right to privacy, awarding "everyone [...] the right to privacy in their private and family life and in their home, and in relation to their mail and telecommunications" and that "the right to be protected against the misuse of their personal data" (Federal Constitution of the Swiss Confederation 1999).

Aiming at bringing the Federal Law on the Surveillance of Postal and Telecommunications Traffic (Federal Assembly of the Swiss Confederation 2000) into line with the recent technological developments, the Federal Council's draft proposal explicitly includes the Internet, namely Internet telephony and emails (Swiss Federal Data Protection Commissioner 2010/2011). The draft proposal (Swiss Federal Data Protection Commissioner 2010/2011), in principle, authorizes Swiss governmental authorities to use monitoring software, although with narrow limits, to avoid the systematic monitoring in advance. Therefore, the draft proposal intends to set more restrictive conditions for the surveillance of a suspect's computer using Trojans compared to the regular telephone and Internet surveillance. In addition to the previous order by a public prosecutor and a judicial approval the employment of Trojans requires as further condition the prosecution of offences meeting the qualifications for an undercover investigation (Fontana 2011).

Beyond that, the draft reduces the surveillance to encrypted transmitted data like mails or communication via Skype; the recording of passwords, searching of hard discs or room monitoring by accessing a computer's microphone and camera are not included (Fontana 2011; Schaffner 2011). Since the draft proposal is expected to come into force only within the next two or three years, the legal situation currently remains unclear.

In addition to the pending revision of the Federal Law on the Surveillance of Postal and Telecommunications Traffic the Swiss Federal Council announced amendments[61] to the Regulation on the Surveillance of Postal and Telecommunications Traffic (Swiss Federal Council 2001) to clarify which Internet Service Providers would obliged to deliver data to Swiss law enforcement authorities.

---

61 The Swiss Federal Council implemented the revised Regulation on the Surveillance of Post and Telecommunications Traffic starting January 1, 2012, see http://www.admin.ch/aktuell/00089/index.html?lang=de&msg-id=42332.

According to the revised Regulation the Internet Access Providers are obliged to deliver data to Swiss law enforcement authorities; providers of chats or blogs only and providers of private networks are exempted from this duty (Swiss Federal Data Protection Commissioner 2010/2011).

4.4.2.2 Austria

Reportedly, the program has also been sold to State agencies in Austria (Bobi 2011). According to Digitask, the developer of the Bundestrojaner,[62] Austrian government authorities at least once acquired a highly controversial computer program, in that the case the so-called "Remote Forensic Software" (Bobi 2011; Austrian Federal Ministry of Justice 2008, p. 15).

Current findings point to the fact that Austrian authorities illegally used the control and monitoring software. The monitoring of message-related computer applications like Email or Voice over Internet Protocols (VoIP) can take place in conformity with the law but enabling the software's user to enter the targeted computer by use of Trojans to investigate the computer from the outside, therewith accomplishing an online surveillance, cannot be based on a parent act within Austria (Austrian Federal Ministry of Justice 2008, p. 33).

4.4.3 Concluding Legal Assessment

Even though each individual country has different legal requirements relating to the lawfulness of interceptions[63] and online surveillance,[64] the above described Council of Europe's Convention on Cybercrime[65] can be seen as a guideline for developing internal legislation; in this legal instrument, Article 19 is relevant regarding online surveillance and Articles 20 and 21 deal with interception.

Article 19 of the Convention (Council of Europe 2004)[66] states, that each signatory State "shall adopt such legislative and other measures as may be necessary to empower its competent authorities to search or similarly access a computer system or part of it and computer data stored therein; and a computer-data storage medium in which computer data may be stored in its territory".

Article 20 of the Convention addresses the real-time collection of traffic data. According to Article 21 of the Convention, addressing the interception of content data, among others "each Party shall adopt such legislative and other measures as

[62] See Sect. 4.4.1.2.

[63] See supra note 45.

[64] Commonly a warrant is needed to accomplish a lawful interception or online search.

[65] See Sect. 4.3.3.

[66] Article 19: Search and seizure of stored computer data.

may be necessary, in relation to a range of serious offences to be determined by domestic law, to empower its competent authorities to collect or record through the application of technical means on the territory of that Party and compel a service provider, within its existing technical capability to collect or record through the application of technical means on the territory of that Party, or to co-operate and assist the competent authorities in the collection or recording of, content data, in real-time, of specified communications in its territory transmitted by means of a computer system [...]".

Giving online surveillance and interceptions a solid legal basis is expected to contribute to the freedom and fundamental rights of each individual citizen. Adopting legislative measures to empower the competent authorities contributes to stable jurisprudence and to provide legal certainty. To date several countries which have signed the Convention still lack of any explicit reference; accordingly there are still efforts needed to satisfactory fulfill the Convention on Cybercrime.

4.5 Enforcement of Copyright

In parallel to the augmented use of the globally available World Wide Web as communication tool, illegal activities and/or preliminary measures thereto increasingly shift from the real into the online world and concomitant among others a new field of activity for copyright infringements appeared on the scene, namely within file-sharing sites and on Internet marketplaces like eBay. Internet users among others download music illegally by simultaneously putting them on the market or use copyright reserved picture files within the frame of (private or commercial) Internet auctions. Supported by the existing and above described opportunities to act anonymously on the Internet[67] copyright infringers to a great extent get away without punishment.[68]

Within the last years repeatedly (beginning with the famous Napster case at the beginning of this century) corresponding Internet portals emerged (and for the most part disappeared a little while later), like the recently blocked online storage and file delivery service "Megaupload.com" or the German website "kino.to".

"Kino.to" was a German-speaking video on demand website for cinematographic works, television series and TV reports best-known for copying and viewing pirated audiovisual content.[69] Held and controlled by anonymous users the website's access was blocked due to violations of copyright law in June 2011.

---

[67] See Sect. 2.2.

[68] In recent years a number of attorneys specialized on copyright law whereby the dispatch of cease-and-desist letters increased.

[69] The purpose of "Kino.to" was to collect links to attractive audiovisual content and to promote these links at the website next to advertisements. These advertisements to a great extent contained illegal material themselves, such as links to destructive software or deceptive web services; for further details see Moeller 2011.

Up to its shut down by German authorities the website was told to be one of the 50 most popular German websites.

In the case of the storage service "Megaupload.com" on January 19, 2012, US Federal authorities shut down one of the Internet's most popular websites as part of an indictment accusing the operators of the website of running an international criminal organisation allowing Internet participants to easily watch or share pirated content of numerous types of copyrighted works (Horwitz and Kang 2012). According to a statement of the US Justice Department "this action is among the largest criminal copyright cases ever brought by the United States" since "the estimated harm caused by the conspiracy's criminal conduct to copyright holder is well in excess of $500 million" (US Department of Justice 2012).

Immediately after the website's shutdown and the arrest of seven executives including the company's founder,[70] the activists of "Anonymous"[71] announced revenge in the form of an "operation payback"[72] and threatened to take several popular websites offline, among others of the Federal Bureau of Investigation (FBI), the US Department of Justice and the Motion Pictures Association of America (Horwitz and Kang 2012). Shortly afterwards, "Anonymous" carried out their threats by temporarily shutting down ten websites, among them the US Department of Justice's website, with a distributed denial of service attack (DDoS)[73] (Ralph 2012). For this purpose, a large number of activists using Low Orbit Ion Cannon (LOIC)[74] simultaneously sent network traffic like senseless Internet inquiries to the targeted website(s) and therewith (in that event) overloaded the Department of Justice's website.

Related to the augmented emergence of file-sharing sites etc. and the therein committed copyright infringements a new field of activity for lawyers emerged and, accordingly, in recent years a number of attorneys specialized on copyright law. Even though in the course of the increasing dispatch of cease-and-desist letters the awareness of Internet copyright infringements has increased a little, many Internet participants still held copyright infringements of being only trivial offences.

With regard to these conflicting opinions it is still to be clarified whose "right" prevails, the privacy of the respective file-sharer trying to hide his identity by acting anonymously within the World Wide Web or the right holders' copyright and consequently their demand for gathering information from the Internet Service Providers about violators by disclosure of the used IP addresses for enforcing their rights.

---

70 "Megaupload.com" is led by Kim Dotcom, formerly known as Kim Schmitz or Kim Tim Jim Vestor, a German entrepreneur living in Auckland, New Zealand, and having his place in business in Hong Kong.

71 See supra note 20.

72 Anonymous' "operation payback" describes a decentralized and coordinated group of attacks on opponents of Internet piracy and pro-copyright organisations starting in 2010.

73 See Sect. 2.1.3.

74 LOIC is an open source network stress testing and denial-of-service attack application.

According to the latest jurisdiction of the Court of Appeal of the Swiss canton Berne, IP addresses collected by a private firm using discovery software are to be considered as illegally "acquired" (Weber 2011c, pp. 28/29) and may not be used for Internet participants' identification (Berne Court of Appeal 2011). In this particular case,[75] a holder of rights in music titles filed a criminal complaint with the prosecution authorities on the basis of 531 IP addresses collected by a private firm, potentially belonging to persons having illegally downloaded music titles. The copyright holder asked the authorities to request from the relevant Internet Service Providers disclosure of the Internet users' real names and addresses belonging to these IP addresses. The authorities imposed a cost advance on the complainant arguing that the request would mainly serve the enforcement of civil law rights.

The Court held that the complainant would mainly be interested in gathering evidence for the enforcement of civil law rights based on an alleged violation of Copyright Law through the criminal prosecution. Irrespective of the question whether such procedural step would be justified the Court of Appeal expressed the opinion that at first instance the legality of collecting the 531 IP addresses by a private firm had to be assessed. Thereby, the Court of Appeal relied on the *Logistep* decision[76] of the Swiss Federal Court of 8 September 2010 indicating that Copyright Law may not enjoy a higher value than Data Protection Law (Swiss Federal Court 2010).[77] According to the Swiss Federal Court, private (economic) interests in having others complying with Copyright Law cannot outweigh the interest of an individual in having his/her data protected from being disclosed; data protection includes an element of public interest and, therefore, prevails under the given circumstances. Consequently, information gained and collected by a private firm in relation to IP addresses without the consent of the concerned individual is to be considered as illegally "required" information and may not be used as evidence in proceedings, unless a specific exemption applies.

Summarizing, on the one side Internet users participating in peer-to-peer-networks[78] sites argue that their IP addresses are tantamount to personal data and therewith are in need of protection since Copyright Law may not enjoy a higher value than Data Protection Law (Weber 2011b, pp. 191/192). Right holders on the other side fear for the violation of their rights by simultaneously feeling incapable to protect their "property" and due to that seek for the divulgence of the used IP addresses, if necessary with the aid of specialized business models.

---

[75] The subsequent passage is partly based on Weber 2011c.

[76] The business model of Logistep AG, a Swiss enterprise, consists in collecting IP addresses of Internet users who participate in P2P networks and make available works, protected by Copyright Law, to third persons without having the copyright holder's permission. Acting (at least indirectly) on behalf of the right holders Logistep delivers the respective IP addresses to the prosecutors in criminal proceedings enabling them to request from the relevant Internet Service Providers the disclosure of the name of the respective Internet participant; for more detailed information see Weber 2011b.

[77] In that case both static and dynamic IP addresses were qualified as personal data.

[78] See Sect. 2.2.2.

Regarding this issue, Article 10 para 1 of the Convention of Cybercrime[79] might be of interest, stating that "each party shall adopt such legislative and other measures as may be necessary to establish as criminal offences under its domestic law the infringement of copyright [...] where such acts are committed willfully, on a commercial scale and by means of a computer system" (Council of Europe 2004). Since this Convention's provision makes commercial scale a condition and a substantial percentage of Internet participants committing copyright infringements (by among others using file-sharing sites etc.) are private persons the Convention of Cybercrime does not concern these infringements.

References

Austrian Federal Ministry of Justice (2008) Final report of the Austrian working group on online surveillance. 9 April 2008. http://www.webinformation.at/material/AG_OnlineDurchsuchung_Endbericht.pdf. Accessed 31 Jan 2012

Barlow JP (1996) A declaration of the independence of cyberspace. 9 February 1996. http://w2.eff.org/Censorship/Internet_censorship_bills/barlow_0296.declaration. Accessed 31 Jan 2012

Berne Court of Appeal (2011) Decision of 22 March 2011. Canton of Berne. http://www.grundrechte.ch/2011/og_bk_11_9. Accessed 31 Jan 2012

Bobi E (2011) Trojanische Sitten: Der Bundestrojaner wurde ohne rechtliche Grundlage eingesetzt. profil online. 22 October 2011. http://www.profil.at/articles/1142/560/310153/bundestrojaner-trojanische-sitten. Accessed 31 Jan 2012

Braun F, Roggenkamp JD (2011) 0zapftis—(Un)Zulässigkeit von "Staatstrojanern". Kommunikation Recht 11:681–686

Chaos Computer Club (2011) Chaos computer club analyzes government malware. 8 October 2011. http://ccc.de/en/updates/2011/staatstrojaner. Accessed 31 Jan 2012.(CCC 2011a)

Chaos Computer Club (2011) Bylaw. http://www.ccc.de/en/satzung. Accessed 31 Jan 2012. (CCC 2011b)

Chaos Computer Club (2011) Analyse einer Regierungs-Malware. 8 October 2011. http://www.ccc.de/system/uploads/76/original/staatstrojaner-report23.pdf. Accessed 31 Jan 2012. (CCC 2011c)

Chaos Computer Club (2011) Chaos computer club analyzes new German government spyware. 26 October 2011. http://www.ccc.de/en/updates/2011/analysiert-aktueller-staatstrojaner. Accessed 31 Jan 2012. (2011d)

Chaos Computer Club (2011) 0zapftis—Teil 2, Analyse einer Regierungs-Malware: Drei Jahre sind in der IT eine wirklich lange Zeit. 26 October 2011. http://www.ccc.de/system/uploads/83/original/staatstrojaner-report42.pdf. Accessed 31 Jan 2012. (CCC 2011e)

Chaos Computer Club (2011) Chaos computer club analysiert aktuelle Version des Staatstrojaners. 26 October 2011. http://www.ccc.de/de/updates/2011/analysiert-aktueller-staatstrojaner. Accessed 31 Jan 2012. (CCC 2011f)

Cottier T, Delimatsis P, Diebold NF (2008) Article XIV GATS. In: Wolfrum R, Stoll PT, Feinäugle C (eds) WTO—Trade in services. Martinus Nijhoff Publishers, Leiden and Boston

Council of Europe (1950) European convention for the protection of human rights and fundamental freedoms. 4 November 1950. http://conventions.coe.int/treaty/Commun/QueVoulezVous.asp?NT=005&CL=ENG. Accessed 31 Jan 2012

[79] See Sect. 4.3.3.

Council of Europe (2004) Convention on cybercrime. 23 Nov 2001. http://conventions.coe.int/Treaty/Commun/QueVoulezVous.asp?NT=185&CM=8&DF=02/06/2010&CL=ENG. Accessed 31 Jan 2012
Council of Europe (2006) The additional protocol to the convention on cybercrime, concerning the criminalization of acts of a racist and xenophobic nature committed through computer systems. http://conventions.coe.int/treaty/Commun/QueVoulezVous.asp?NT=189&CL=ENG. Accessed 31 Jan 2012
Council of the European Union (2001) Council framework decision of 28 May 2001 combating fraud and counterfeiting of non-cash means of payment. http://eur-lex.europa.eu/LexUriServ/LexUriServ.do?uri=OJ:L:2001:149:0001:0004:EN:PDF. Accessed 31 Jan 2012
Council of the European Union (2005) Council framework decision 2005/222/JHA of 24 February 2005 on attacks against information systems. http://eur-lex.europa.eu/LexUriServ/LexUriServ.do?uri=OJ:L:2005:069:0067:0071:EN:PDF. Accessed 31 Jan 2012
Council of the European Union (2008) Amendment of the framework decision on combating terrorism. 18 April 2008. http://europa.eu/rapid/pressReleasesAction.do?reference=MEMO/08/255. Accessed 31 Jan 2012
European Parliament (1995) Directive 95/46/EC of the European parliament and of the council of 24 October 1995 on the protection of individuals with regard to the processing of personal data and on free movement of such data. http://eur-lex.europa.eu/LexUriServ/LexUriServ.do?uri=OJ:L:1995:281:0031:0050:EN:PDF. Accessed 31 Jan 2012
Federal Assembly of the Swiss Confederation (2000) Federal Law on the surveillance of post and telecommunications traffic. SR780.1. http://www.admin.ch/ch/d/sr/780_1/index.html. Accessed 31 Jan 2012
Federal Constitution of the Swiss Confederation (1999) SR 101. http://www.admin.ch/ch/e/rs/101/index.html. Accessed 31 Jan 2012
Fontana K (2011) Enge Grenzen für "Trojaner". Neue Zürcher Zeitung. No. 275. 24 Nov 2011: 12
Gercke M (2011) 10 years convention on cybercrime: achievements and failures of the council of europe's instrument in the fight against internet-related crimes. Comput Law Rev Int 5:142–149
German Federal Constitutional Court (2008) 1 BvR 370/07, 1 BvR 595/07. 27 February 2008. http://www.bverfg.de/entscheidungen/rs20080227_1bvr037007.html. Accessed 31 Jan 2012
Graham J, Howard R, Olson R (eds) (2011) Cyber security essentials. Auerbach Publications, Boca Raton
High-Level Experts Group (HLEG) (2008) Report of the chairman of HLEG. 3 September 2008. http://www.itu.int/osg/csd/cybersecurity/gca/docs/Report_of_the_Chairman_of_HLEG_to_ITU_SG_03_sept_08.pdf. Accessed 31 Jan 2012
Horwitz S, Kang C (2012) Federal indictment claims popular Web site Megaupload.com shared pirated material. The Washington Post. 20 January 2012. http://www.washingtonpost.com/business/economy/federal-indictment-claims-popular-web-site-shared-pirated-material/2012/01/19/gIQA4rDwBQ_print.html. Accessed 31 Jan 2012
International Telecommunication Union (ITU) (2007) Global cybersecurity agenda: framework for international cooperation in cybersecurity. http://www.ifap.ru/library/book169.pdf. Accessed 31 Jan 2012
Jackson M (2011) Right to privacy, unlawful search and surveillance. In: Chan J, Lim CL (eds) Law of the Hong Kong constitution. Sweet and Maxwell, Hong Kong
Moore R (2011) Cybercrime: investigating high-technology computer crime, 2nd edn. Anderson Publishing, Burlington
Munin N (2010) Legal guide to GATS. Kluwer Law International, The Netherlands
Ralph T (2012) Hacker collective anonymous shuts down department of justice website, among others. GlobalPost. 19 January 2012. http://www.globalpost.com/dispatch/news/business-tech/technology-news/120119/anonymous-hacks-DOJ-universal-websites-megaupload. Accessed 31 Jan 2012

Rosenbach M, Stark H, Winter S (2011) The shady past of Germany's Spyware. Spiegel online international. 17 October 2011. http://www.spiegel.de/international/germany/0,1518,792276,00.html. Accessed 31 Jan 2012

Ryga BM (1995) Cyberporn: Contemplating the first amendment in cyberspace. Seton Hall Const Law J 6:221–223

Schaffner D (2011) Sommaruga setzt der Überwachung im Internet nun Grenzen. Tagesanzeiger. 24 Nov 2011: 4

Schefer M (2001) Die Kerngehalte von Grundrechten: Geltung, Dogmatik, inhaltliche Ausgestaltung. Stämpfli, Berne

Schjølberg S, Ghernaouti-Hélie S (2011) Potential new global legal mechanisms on combating cybercrime and global cyberattacks. A presentation at the ISPAC International Conference on Cybercrime: Global Phenomenon and its Challenges. 2–4 December 2011. http://cybercrimelaw.net/documents/ISPAC.pdf. Accessed 31 Jan 2012

Solove DJ (2007) The Future of Reputation: Gossip, Rumor, and Privacy on the Internet. Yale University Press, New Haven

Swiss Federal Council (2001) Regulation on the surveillance of post and telecommunications traffic. SR.780.11. http://www.admin.ch/ch/d/sr/780_11/index.html. Accessed 31 Jan 2012

Swiss Federal Court (2010) Decision of 8 September 2010. http://jumpcgi.bger.ch/cgi-bin/JumpCGI?id=08.09.2010_1C_285/2009. Accessed 31 Jan 2012

Swiss Federal Data Protection Commissioner (2010/2011) Progress report 18: revision of the federal law on the surveillance of post and telecommunications traffic. http://www.edoeb.admin.ch/dokumentation/00445/00509/01732/01753/index.html?lang=de. Accessed 31 Jan 2012

Tschentscher A (2011) Computer-Grundrecht gegen "Staatstrojaner". Neue Zürcher Zeitung. 9 Nov 2011: 21

United Nations (1966) International covenant on civil and political rights. 16 December 1966. http://www2.ohchr.org/english/law/ccpr.htm. Accessed 31 Jan 2012

United States Department of Justice (2012) Justice department charges leaders of megaupload with widespread online copyright infringement. Office of Public Affairs. 19 January 2012. http://www.justice.gov/opa/pr/2012/January/12-crm-074.html. Accessed 31 Jan 2012

Weber RH, Sommerhalder M (2007) Das Recht der personenbezogenen Information. Schulthess/Nomos, Zurich

Weber RH (2008) Grundrecht auf Vertraulichkeit und Integrität. Digma 2:94–97

Weber RH (2009) Internet governance: regulatory challenges. Schulthess, Zurich

Weber RH (2011a) The right to be forgotten: more than a Pandora's Box? J Intellect Property Inf Technol E-Commer Law 2:120–130 (Weber 2011a)

Weber RH (2011b) Switzerland: private use of discovery software for IP addresses. Comput Law Rev Int 6:191–192 (Weber 2011b)

Weber RH (2011c) Legality of IP-address discovery software—Logistep. Comput Law Rev Int 1:28–29 (Weber 2011c)

Weber RH, Wolf CA, Heinrich UI (2012) Neue Brennpunkte im Verhältnis von Informationstechnologien, Datensammlungen und flexibilisierter Rechtsordnung. Jusletter. 12 March 2012. http://jusletter.weblaw.ch/article/de/_10019. Accessed 11 April 2012

Wildhaber L, Breitenmoser S (1992) Art. 8 EMRK. In: Golsong H, Karl W (eds) Internationaler Kommentar zur Europäischen Menschenrechtskommission. Commentary. Carl Heymanns Verlag, Cologne

Chapter 5
Outlook

At the beginning of the Internet era partly the perception of a new world without legal borders prevailed since the medium Internet is of a virtual nature and technical monitoring possibilities by State authorities seemed to be difficult to obtain. Meanwhile, this assessment has fundamentally changed; the World Wide Web is as regulated as the traditional world and the exercise of freedoms did not become much easier.

In view of these developments the existence of a right to act anonymously on the Internet by using anonymization is still hotly debated, especially with regard to recent events like the shutdown of "Megaupload.com", the disclosure of the Trojan (horse) software used by the German government, the countless hacker attacks of activists like "Anonymous"[1] or the ongoing debate about the existence of a right to be forgotten.[2]

Even though a review of the international legal framework has shown that a right to act anonymously on the Internet is not explicitly included in legal instruments so far there is no evidence that such a right should not be part of the widely acknowledged right to keep certain personal data confidential, particularly due to the described correlation between the anonymity and the fundamental right to privacy. The legally consolidated protection of private life, home and correspondence of Internet participants pleads for the existence of a right of not being totally monitored; in fact, States have the obligation to create an environment free of surveillance by improving the existing legislative frameworks. However, a right to rely on anonymity cannot be without limits since State interests do exist, justifying governmental intervention into the sphere of individuals. In order to avoid the individual protection regime's weakening the respective rules, allowing interventions, must be interpreted in a narrow way.

[1] See Chap. 2, footnote 6.
[2] See Sect. 3.2.2.3.

R. H. Weber and U. I. Heinrich, *Anonymization*, SpringerBriefs in Cybersecurity,
DOI: 10.1007/978-1-4471-4066-5_5, © The Author(s) 2012

MIX
Papier aus verantwortungsvollen Quellen
Paper from responsible sources
FSC® C105338

If you have any concerns about our products,
you can contact us on
ProductSafety@springernature.com

In case Publisher is established outside the EU,
the EU authorized representative is:
Springer Nature Customer Service Center GmbH
Europaplatz 3, 69115 Heidelberg, Germany

Printed by Libri Plureos GmbH
in Hamburg, Germany